To Mother,

from

Katharine and Hugh.

Christmas. 1948

MORNING, NOON AND NIGHT IN LONDON

MORNING, NOON AND NIGHT IN LONDON

BY

SACHEVERELL SITWELL

LONDON
MACMILLAN & CO. LTD
1948

COPYRIGHT

LIST OF PLATES

Note. The centre figure in this drawing is described
out of its place, as it has been transferred from
"Haymarket 2^h du matin" described on p. 80.

TO
THE OCCUPANT
OF THE PRIVATE HANSOM

As I take up my pen, in August 1944, the streets of London are in daily and nightly peril from the flying bombs. When you, the reader, turn these pages that danger may be past, may be gone for ever, but remember that at the time of writing there was no certainty what would be left standing.

This is the hour, I thought, in which to take a walk in London, in imagination, for I live in the country. It is the golden harvest here, the ripe cornfields are cut into like honeycombs. I hear sounds of reaping on the still August air. The only reminder of War, visible or audible, comes from the incessant aeroplanes. But in London . . . It is, as I have said, the day and hour to think of London. A cloudless August morning that already, since I began, is turning into the perfect August afternoon. And it shall remain, for the time being — double summer time or no — at half-past three or four o'clock, an eternal August afternoon in London, in which we lose ourselves, and the next moment we are wondering if we have been dreaming.

For we are walking up the dark arcade behind His Majesty's, one of the forgotten corners of old London ; we pass Burgess, the hairdresser's, and look at the dusty bottles of Bay Rum in his windows, and under its glass shade, at the wax bust of the young fop of the 'sixties, with Dundreary whiskers. And so, out into the heat and light after that small experience which, I write for myself, is enough to start me dreaming. We are writing, we have resolved, for all persons, young and old, who love London. And we are walking up Lower Regent Street to capture the genius loci of the town.

We may find, not to our surprise, that it is the emanation of its theatres and its music halls. Those are the mirrors that reflect its character. What we see, therefore, are shadows, but in all their colour : men and women of an August afternoon, for we have written that it is eternal, but of seventy or eighty years ago. It is long enough since, that no one, now alive, can contradict. Yet it is here and now, this living moment. I am thinking, as I walk, of the last time I went to His Majesty's, in the August of last year, when *The Merry Widow* was playing. The music of Lehar, a composer whose mind worked naturally and spontaneously in Viennese waltz time, is ringing in my ears, and I cross the street into a patch of shadow. The spell has begun to work. I can remember 1907 ; and how, after my operation for appendicitis, the nurses in the nursing home talked of nothing but *The Merry Widow*. I was ten years old. We are half-way, already, more or less, to 1864. And in another moment, banishing those banal tunes, we have reached it, knowing it, at once, from the difference in the sights and sounds and smells.

And we turn to the left down Piccadilly.

But it is empty of traffic. There are neither horses nor pedestrians. It is only, at present, a painted drop scene, like that view of Holborn Viaduct when Little Tich came on to sing his grocer's song. We could almost be waiting for him to dance on the ends of his long shoes, that were like a pair of stilts. It is unreal when we cross again in front of St James's Church, and meet not a living soul, and are at the corner of Old Bond Street. But it is nothing mysterious. There have been no alerts, nor sirens. We have warned, already, and will explain more fully later, that we are to meet the living, but in their several sorts, so that actual persons of the time will be rubbing shoulders with the travesties and caricatures of seventy or eighty years ago. It is a convention imposed upon us by our guide, but the time has not yet come to call him by his name. That name, in any case, would mean little or nothing, for we have been able to discover little more about him than his name.

And, suddenly, we feel an imminence. We know that someone is about to appear upon the empty scene. It is as hot as on the hottest night in the most crowded theatre. It is, even, the same degree and kind of heat, although this is the August afternoon and the strong sunlight, the place and hour for a long cool drink in the middle of a summer afternoon. The first blackberries will soon be ripe upon the hedges. The fields will be white with mushrooms. In a fortnight it will be September.

Meanwhile, it is a hot spell in August and the town seems empty. You can feel the heat of the pavement through your shoes. It is of large, old paving stones, but the street itself would appear to be of cobbles. Bond Street is paved with cobbles. That is one important difference. There is no asphalt, and there are no motors. In their place a hansom cab, the gondola of the London streets, clop-clops quickly by. The ubiquitous top hat appears at horseback level, and on the box seat of every carriage and every horsedrawn vehicle. Insensibly, the street is filling. The pavement is crowded with persons, and coming towards us in a little empty space that he has to himself, due to his own importance and to the deference of the onlookers, we meet *The Bond Street Beau*.

How many persons of character have strolled along this street, but we may be inclined to think he is the most important of them all ! With the alteration of a mere word or two, we quote the phrase of his contemporary, that : " One at least among the pedestrians along Bond Street sees more spectres arise out of the pavement as he passes the modern buildings than ever stirred the imagination of the passers-by of eighty years ago ".[1] For he is, most certainly, the spectre of that pavement. We could argue that, in comparison, there is none other. For ourselves, he haunts both sides of Bond Street from Conduit Street to Piccadilly.

Even as we write these words, he looms up larger than life in front of the painted drop scene. For, one moment, it is actually Old Bond Street, and the next, it is a painted ' drop ' that he takes with him to all the music halls. We see him as though in the glare and prominence of the foot-lights ; standing before us ; or must conclude that, this August afternoon, he is walking down Bond Street in order to appear in person and be recognized. To be precise, he is standing still. He is at that moment of his performance when he has walked on and is about to sing his song. There is a comparable moment in Spanish dancing, only it comes at the end and not the beginning of the dance ; " at the ninth measure, when the dancers remain motionless and we only hear the grinding of the guitar ". We have written, elsewhere, " that the dancers, at the last note of the guitar, keep, as if petrified, to their positions, in catalepsis of the dance ". And so it is with *The Bond Street Beau*. It is a cata-lepsis induced, of course, by a different sort of music. Bond Street is now crowded ; but that has nothing to do with the music of the crowd motif from *Carmen*, a Spanish rhythm that none but the spiritually and mentally deaf can hear without a stirring of the blood and a tingling of the skin. Instead, we have to imagine the typical rhythms of *Burlington Bertie*, of *The Man who broke the Bank at Monte Carlo* (nephew, surely, in time and disposition to *The Bond Street Beau*, for he belonged to the next generation), and of the songs of Vesta

[1] *The Life and Reminiscences of E. L. Blanchard*, London, Hutchinson & Co., 1891.

Tilley. Rhythms that suggest the inimitable walk of Vesta Tilley up and down the stage, before the footlights ; tunes that, as we recall them, give so much more of the character of London and its inhabitants than will ever emerge in the music of more serious composers.

The Bond Street Beau stands before us in the summer afternoon and occupies, in every sense, the centre of the stage. This pavement is his beat. It is the west side of the street ; the right side as you walk down towards Piccadilly. Of course, if you look at his portrait through the back of the page, you will see him facing in another direction, but, nevertheless, he is for ever coming down Bond Street towards the Piccadilly end. We are to infer that he appears, always, before this painted scene, with the same row of shops opposite, across the street. But for our benefit, this afternoon, we behold him in real life against the living background of his song.

He has come a step nearer. He is within a few feet of us, as though we are in the front row of the stalls. And, indeed, when our eyes look up at him, they are on a level with his waist. Yet we are on the pavement. We are not sitting in the music hall. Perhaps, on occasion, he comes on without any scene at all to sing his song. We shall discover, later, how the artist varies in his treatment according to mood and inspiration ; sometimes giving the actor in a setting of real life ; upon the stage of the theatre against the slanting boards ; or in a symposium of words and actions from the song. It is sufficient if we note, for the moment, that the artist must have studied him many dozens of times in order to present him to us, exactly, as he came on to sing his song.

He is so near to us, now, that he could not come another step forward without knocking into us. And he has no need to. He is at the edge of the footlights. He is posing for his portrait at the moment when the music stops ; and this instant we shall hear him speak, and his music will strike up again. But, all the time, he is a living person and it is our imagination that is at fault for thinking of him in the theatre. He is in the blazing sunlight. We see the shadow of his tasselled walking stick. It is a line of shadow that attaches to the ferrule of his walking stick as that touches on the pavement, and that will move with it if he so much as lifts his hand. His stick casts its own shadow, and it would be difficult to exaggerate the importance of that tasselled wand. In the company he keeps, that is to say his audience, it is a piece of impertinence to come on with a walking stick. They have never seen such a fop or beau in real life, except in Bond Street or in Rotten Row. In his other hand he holds a half-smoked cigar. And he is wearing gloves. A pair of well-made, tight-fitting chamois leather gloves — or are they grey kid ? — for we cannot be quite certain, but we can see the lines of black braid, like the black keys of a keyboard, upon the backs of his knuckles, and disappearing into his cuffs.

The Bond Street Beau wears a top hat, worn at a rakish angle, an eyeglass in his right eye, and cuts so extravagant and withal immaculate a figure that we cannot but examine him from head to foot. We are not alone in our intention. Behind him, two women, who cannot be ladies, or they would not be walking down Bond Street at this hour of the afternoon, still less pausing in conversation on the kerbstone, are discussing this paragon who has passed them by, going over him from point to point, as impressed as we are ourselves, but, perhaps, a little suspicious of him. They have heard the talk and tittle-tattle. They know him by his reputation. One of them, and by her attitude she is not so familiar with this apparition, this spectre rising from the pavement, looks at him attentively while her companion,

THE BOND ST. BEAU.

who knows him well, confides in her and we may even imagine that the salacious details are coupled with a warning :

> Whene'er I take my walks abroad
>   How many girls I see,
> They whisper he's a duke or lord
>   A prince or else M.P. ;
> Observe that manly Grecian bend,
>   That linen, white as snow,
> To kiss my hand I condescend,
>   Yes ! I'm the Bond Street Beau.

This pair of pedestriennes, who are for evermore turning into Bond Street, or to be observed standing, as now, at the corners of Clifford Street or Old Burlington Street, are dressed much alike, one in red and one in yellow. One of them has a dog on a lead. The other, although it is a hot day in August, wears a muff. They must be fashionably dressed at all costs. They do not wear the crinoline, but their skirts are full and ample with deep fringes at the hem, and decorations that to our eyes, not yet accustomed, resemble heavy curtain cords. Verlaine, describing their less modish sisters at this very time, along less expensive Oxford Street or Regent Street, writes of : " d'exquises miss à la longue jupe de satin groseille, jaspée de boue, tigrée de consommés épandus, trouée de chiures de cigarettes ". But these women of Bond Street have their hair raised, at the back, into high chignons upon which are perched their fashionable hats, thin and boat-shaped, rising over the false hair of the chignon, and topped, each, with a flowing ostrich plume.

A glance is enough at that pair of women upon the pavement. We cannot be mistaken. But *The Bond Street Beau* strikes such an attitude. He stands, as though petrified before us in the characteristic moment of his promenade. His weight is on his left heel. He leans on his walking stick

7

and his body is pulled up and held back, stiffly, by his pose. His right foot is forward and he is about to take another step. But where are we to begin ; from his tall hat, or his pointed boots ? We do neither. We start from his waist, which is thrown forward by his attitude.

He wears a short coat, not a frock coat, and it is cut, or even moulded, to his figure ; fastened in front with a single button, or at most a pair ; cut away, as though it would develop into a tail coat, but stopping short of that upon his hips. Excessively waisted, even, so that it gives prominence to his wide shoulders, with a low opening in front and wearing, of course, a flower in his buttonhole. His coat has a low collar, not like the high collars of the Regency, and its whole effect is swallow-tailed but with the tails cut short, so that we see his trousers to the top trouser button, and behind that, his elegant and thin waist. But the dark brown material of his coat is remarkable, too, for the way his sleeves are cut, fuller than in our time, more like the sleeves of an overcoat but short, and specially designed to show his cuffs. His other arm holding the cigar, rests, not by his side, but lies proudly and languidly upon the Bond Street air. We can even see the black stitching on his glove around his thumb.

His head and neck can be considered, like the tailor's dummy, in one piece. For he has a wide shirt front and a big, flowing tie, heavily-knotted, with broad, flapping ends. The ends are not long enough to be tucked into his waistcoat. They float upon the summer air. The tie, therefore, must be an enormous piece of white silk when it lies upon his dressing table. The shirt collar, too, is loose and summery, but little starched, and in its freedom a relic of an earlier age.

Two long, loose, drooping ends trail down and touch his shoulders. They are the ends of his long moustaches, such as we only see now, once every few years, in a cross-country train, between the rural stations, and we know they must be the moustaches of an old carpenter or saddler, someone who works on his own premises, and can keep to the outworn fashions of his youth, someone, moreover, who has never walked down Bond Street, and would not recognize this pattern of his style, for it has come down so long ago from the West End to the mean streets and to the provinces. The face, above the moustaches, is pink and white, very Anglo-Saxon, and unmistakably bleak. The eyeglass in the right eye deprives it of any expression at all but that which is conveyed in the manner in which the entire figure stands.

It is a yellow, corn-coloured moustache and the hair is yellow, too, but elaborately curled and frizzled with the hot tongs, and made stiff with bear's grease which is the fashionable pomade and forms the most common article to be purchased at the hairdresser's, but in our time has disappeared entirely from the counter. Above that, his tall hat has curving brims, a narrow band, nothing but a flat edge over his eyes, and then we see the boat-like sides of it riding on his curls, and the tall crown of his silk hat, more shaped than the top hat of our own time, but in an age when it is universal, when it is worn by kings and beggars, the top hat changes from year to year, besides which, there are top hats for summer or winter, for business or pleasure, and wider knowledge would impute to the top hat as many forms and meanings as to the Turkish or the Persian turban. But, for further information, we will delay until we can arrange a visit to the hatter's.

But what of the Beau's trousers, for we have scarcely mentioned them ! In colour they are a light strawberry roan. We can see the flecks in them. They are of a heavy material which will not crease, which depends upon its cut and fit, not made with turned-up ends, but the foot of the trouser is full-bottomed. It comes forward, nearly touches the pavement at his heels, and covers half his boots, which are elegantly pointed, but have square ends. His trousers, even, may be regarded in three lengths, to the knee, to the ankle, and to where they reach the ground. Now we comprehend the Beau again, as do the two women behind him, in a general glance and it is a surprise, almost, that the traffic takes no notice of him. An old gentleman in top hat, frilled shirt front, short coat, and braided trousers, rides past ; a hansom cab is passing by in the other direction ; we see across Bond Street the typical London stucco houses that stand above the shops ; and immediately in front, only a step away and you could touch it with your hand, one of the old London street posts, familiar objects that tell us it is London and no other town, and which are nothing else than naval guns from the old wooden warships, with the Royal cyphers G.IV or W.IV embossed upon them.

We stand transfixed, quite dumb, before this apparition and it is indeed a moment of time made eternal, for he never passes by. He never takes another step. We are not to have the opportunity of looking back at him over our shoulder. That view of him is the privilege of the two ladies who linger in permanence upon the pavement, and we know from their glances that they agree with us. Ladies and Gentlemen, this is *The Bond Street Beau*! We are within a minute's stroll of Savile Row which is the capital of the world's tailoring. That is the purport or meaning of this ghost who stands before us.

But the well-dressed man, more often than not, has debts. He lives on credit. The cut of his coat and trousers is no clue to the money in his pocket. Could we accompany this splendid figure to the corner, and follow him all through his promenade, we should find that he takes a meal, like humbler persons, in the public house or oyster bar. He is well known in Maiden Lane and Covent Garden, among the other actors. He is a mirror held up to the man of fashion. The reflection is true, but this spectre of Bond Street has to be extreme in order to be typical. And on Sunday afternoon, when Bond Street is deserted, where should we find him ? He will be resting in his lodgings, and his Bond Street clothes will be hanging in his dressing-room, down at the theatre. In fact, he is a comedian aping the man of fashion. Not only this, but the original is so exceedingly curious in himself. Look at him again, and you will see that his moustaches are like a pair of handlebars ! Not for many centuries has this been the fashion. There are knights and barons on the mediaeval tombs with those moustaches, but this beau with his top hat and curled hair, and his companions whom we are to meet, are more far-fetched than any of the fops in history.

Let *The Bond Street Beau* be our introduction to this town of swells and dandies ! But it is not all pleasure. Thieves and pickpockets mingle with the crowd as the late afternoon becomes another August night. There are all those hours before us until three o'clock in the morning, when we stand in the Haymarket, near to where we started. We will have a momentary, and last, vision of women in green and blue crinolines, smoking cigars, with rouged faces, walking along the pavement. . . . It is the Babylon of the nineteenth century, except that, unlike Babylon, it has not fallen. It has been battered, but still stands upright, in pride of which we set out for this stroll or recession, and to spend the August afternoon and evening.

The Bond Street Beau, we know it now, is a comedian and not an actual person. But his walk and attitude are not to be found in the pages of any novelist or historian. His are the characteristics that they do not set out to capture, or that escape them. No full-length biography could tell us as much as this meeting with him upon the pavement. It is because he is living and moving, which never happens, or is only hinted at, in fiction. Music is the secret. It is music to which he walks and moves, and which explains and makes probable his attitude. Could we find ourselves, here and now, not in Bond Street but in the Prater, the movement not only of the crowd but more particularly of the man of fashion, true or false, would be to a different measure, born of the waltz and polka, due to Millocker, Ziehrer, many others, but to mention the immortal Johann Strauss. Popular music can lead, or come last and personify. For London there are the tunes of Bank Holiday, in the gait and accent of the costermongers and of the swings and roundabouts on Hampstead Heath. How else, in our own time and but a few years ago, could the *Lambeth Walk* imitate and put on record the strut and Cockney accent of a small part of London ? That personification, rich or mean, is of the same family as *The Bond Street Beau*; and that ghost, we doubt it not, would know and recognize his descendant from the Lambeth slums.

As he stands before the scene, the crown of his top hat, but it is worn, of course, with the fashionable slant, touches the top storey of the buildings opposite. His figure occupies Bond Street, cellar to attic. He bears down on us. We see him, not from eye level, but over the heads of the orchestra, above the footlights, as we would see him in the music hall. But we must continue on our round. Seeing, but unseen, we bid farewell to this colossus or Atlas. We cross Bond Street, turn into Burlington Gardens, and in a few moments are in Regent Street.

And, suddenly, there is an incident, as we are passing the door of Lewis and Allenby. A beautiful little doorway, with the Royal arms over it, and fluted pilasters to either side. Shop windows at both ends, the iron rail of a balcony above each window ; and down at pavement level each window is finished off with a brass plate that has Lewis and

Allenby upon it, and under that a kind of iron grating a foot or eighteen inches high ending on the pavement. The set, therefore, if we are to imagine it as such, has order and architecture. In the windows hang various garments or lengths of material, and their prices ; while outside the further window, head in air, oblivious, stands a whiskered policeman in his top hat. This ' primitive ' of the London police force takes no action. Or is he a top-hatted footman ?

The persons concerned are two ladies and a gentleman. Behind them, in the doorway of the shop, a little crossing sweeper has run in to give the alarm, and the manager and his assistants come rushing out. But it is easy to read in their vacuous expressions that the thieves or shoplifters will escape. Even so, our vision is static and no detail is lost upon us. Once again, and it is becoming like a signature, one of the old street posts of London is in the foreground. The incident, in fact, hinges upon it. This is the centre of the drama. The gentleman in the foreground is delayed or held up by it, while the two ladies have passed it by and are half-way to safety. But is the gentleman their victim or accomplice ? Perhaps he is the one, while pretending to be the other. He is an elderly man wearing a yellow waistcoat, a blue tail coat, and a grey top hat. He leans forward over the street post, one hand resting on it and holding, like *The Bond Street Beau*, a half-smoked cigar. With the other hand he has snatched up the broom of the crossing sweeper that the boy had left there and is defending himself against the ladies' poodle, which runs off with a stolen bone. Or it could be that he is helping them by adding to the confusion.

His grey top hat, well brushed and glistening, is the pivot of the action. For the street post and the top hat are male emblems, as it were. We look at the black band on his hat, and at his moustache and curls and whiskers. For the incident, really, is entirely feminine.

For now we have, what we never get in any history or work of fiction, two living figures moving before our eyes. A pair of young women in a hurry to get away. The crinoline of the near one flows out behind her and she is not entirely past the street post yet. The gentleman, their friend or dupe, is still involved in it. He is in fascinating propinquity to the crinoline, and the sound of it, as that of the mythical waves in some fretted seashell, must be ringing in his ears. The grot of Venus has opened to him, and on the pavement of Regent Street he could fancy himself for a moment in her scented boudoir. She is a tall young woman, and our first impression is of her dark eyebrows and her hands and feet. She looks back at the gentleman, whether to fascinate him, or to give us or all passers-by the benefit of her glances, we cannot tell ; or it may be concern on her part, to be certain that his attention has been distracted, that her lure has succeeded and she can make away.

She is tall and thin and light of weight, twenty-four or twenty-five years old, we would guess, and good-looking, more than beautiful. But, by some magic of the age, her appearance is calculated, it is fore-ordained, to display the trembling of the crinoline. Certain dancers, according to this rule, are as though born for the short ballet skirt, while others of a different build look awkward in it. The back of her crinoline, like a great wave, eddies against the street post. The more so because the whole back of her dress, from the shoulders down, is a patterned Paisley shawl of green and red. This has an elaborate edging or border, a line of floreations from neck to waist, at which point the pattern spreads across her back, just where the black sleeve of her dress peeps forth. From out of this, with the hem or fringe of the shawl thrown over it, a white cuff emerges, and we see a long thin glove upon her right hand and her fingers that by means of a loop hold up her skirt in front.

KLEPTOMANIA.

From her sleeve and gloved hand, and from her shoulder, flows the crinoline, while the shawl draped over the back of it like shimmering spray imparts the wave-like motion. For the shawl, of course, shakes with a different movement to the crinoline it covers. It is like the pattern of foam upon the hollow of the wave. It slides up, and sinks back, with a silken rustling sound, but the entire movement is that it is pouring down. And we come from the hem of her Paisley shawl to her black skirt, and follow its flounces to where they spring up in a wide curve or outline to her waist, and we see that she is carrying a parcel in her other hand, pressed into her figure, and half hidden by a great mass of gathering up of shawl. In fact she is concealing the parcel, and the cry is shoplifting or *Kleptomania*.

This young woman, whom we admire the more we look at her, to the degree that we feel certain she is innocent and there has been a mistake, has dark hair, straight, and parted in the middle. It is caught up at the back into a deep net or snood, a fashion that may remind us of our own time, for the nymphs of 1939 wore the snood but not the crinoline, and we may picture the Venus of our day in the pose of Titian's Venus, lying naked in her snood, while her gallant, in pyjamas, turns the needle on the radio. But this ghost, for she is another spectre, but rising, this time, from the pavement of Bond Street, wears a hat that is also very near to contemporary fashion. It is a round, flat fur hat, but it is worn straight and covers the whole head. Rising from the front of it there is a round pompom, corresponding exactly to the pompom at the end of the white poodle's tail, and to the pompoms upon its legs above its paws. She has a large clasp, probably a cameo, at her throat ; and we look down her figure to where she holds up the loop upon her skirt, and lifts it to show her petticoat. A white lace petticoat punctured heavily like curtain lace, from which her ankle and foot, as thin as her wrist, emerge in a red stocking and a black bootee.

Her companion, of whom we only see the head and shoulders, presses forward, putting the responsibility upon her friend. She leans her head down and tries to pass quickly by the plate-glass window. All we see of her is the line of her skirt, the upper part of her body, and the stolen package in her hand. She has long fair hair, brushed straight, and flowing out upon her shoulder, lifting up and down as she hurries and nearly breaks into a run. This fair-haired young woman wears neither chignon nor snood. Her hair flows loose and untrammelled. Her hat is in the same fashion as her friend's, not round, but boat-shaped and riding on her hair, with a white plume, an uncurled ostrich feather, flowing out at the back, and taking the same direction as her flowing hair. Her bodice has a woollen net thrown over it, instead of a shawl, taking the place in imagery of the chignon or snood, implying that this Venus, too, can be snared and taken in a net. The wide meshes cling to her bust and shoulders ; but it could be, as she runs past, that we are mistaken and that it is a silken material with the wavering lines of the lattice woven in it. Why is it that the net or lattice enters so often into the symbolism of the women's dresses of the 'sixties ? Looking again at the two young women, all the reliance and character are in the first. She is the one who made the plan, and by the exercise of her charms will have her way. The snake-like coils of her chignon in its netted bag, and her steady glance over her shoulder at the gentleman in the grey top hat, are in contrast to her coquetry in holding up her skirt in front. It is the fashion when walking, and in this manner the front of the crinoline is kept off the pavement ; but there is an art in it, just as there is an art in the way a dancer or an actress will walk across the stage. It is, indeed, the art of walking in a crinoline. We hear at this hot hour, at four o'clock in the afternoon, the sound of the two young women running in their hooped skirts. We behold the lifting and billowing of the crinoline.

But it is not the last we are to see of this young woman. In a few moments we meet her again ; but this time it is *The Dark Girl Dress'd in Blue.* For August in London is timeless. It is yesterday or tomorrow ; or today ; and she may have hurried home to change her dress. A tall, robust young man has passed her and takes off his hat. She looks back at him. In fact the drama between them is played back to back. They are contained and held together by the possibilities in this chance meeting. He is up in London from the country. That much we know immediately from the clothes he wears and from the way he stands. For he is dressed in riding breeches. He wears riding boots with spurs, a black velveteen coat which comes half-way to his knees, and carries a long riding switch under his arm. This coat is only fastened at the collar by the top button, and shows his yellow or buff waistcoat and gold watch chain. He has a blue stock tie with white polka dots, and a red handkerchief in his breast pocket. He lifts his grey top hat. He does not take off his top hat. He only raises it. We see his well-brushed and pomaded hair. He is clean shaven, and this is significant, for it means that he is a particular person with an individuality. He is not as others. In this hirsute age he would be recognized immediately just because of this absence of moustache and whiskers. He lifts his top hat and stands still, waiting. He hopes the episode is not at an end and that he will hear more of it.

Behind him, on the pavement, *The Dark Girl Dress'd in Blue* pauses for a moment. She hesitates ; and that is enough. The next movement is for him to make. She wears the full crinoline and is dressed from head to foot in blue. An enormous crinoline and of delphinium blue. For ourselves, and how much more for those who lived and moved then, we cannot see the monstrous bell of a crinoline, like a blue bell-flower, without thinking of the pistils and stamen in its circumference. We would see the fitting of the crinoline and that moment when she climbs into the cage, when it closes round her. The enchantment comes from the interior secrets, so carefully hidden, and to which so much attention has been drawn. That is why the lifting of the front of the crinoline is such an attraction. There was the fashion, a year or two earlier, for short hooped skirts that did not reach the ground, and we could have seen ladies with walking sticks picking their way like sea birds, far out, at the margin of the sands. But *The Dark Girl Dress'd in Blue* wears the extreme crinoline that sweeps the pavement. Her smooth back reminds us of a maid's or nurse's dress, for we have never seen a young woman in day clothes, dressed from head to heel. A blue lace shawl, of darker blue, is draped from her sleeves over the entire back of the crinoline, dividing it into two zones of a lighter and a darker blue. It is like the shading or veining of the delphinium. She wears a white bonnet touched up and lined with blue, a bonnet that has artificial flowers, in blue, in its brim above her forehead ; while in her right hand, from her full blue sleeve, her white glove with a blue ribbon at her wrist holds up a parasol, like a little white canopy with blue embroidery upon it.

She turns and half looks back at him. That is to say, she stares at ourselves and we notice, curiously, that he is facing us and that though he gazes in her direction his glances, really and truly, are for our benefit. Both Harry Clifton and Kate Harley, who is *The Dark Girl Dress'd in Blue*, are asking for our verdict upon them. Are they feigning an interest in each other ? Can it be a double

turn ? Another primitive policeman, tophatted, crosses
the street on to the pavement in the background. He is as
oblivious of what is happening as the policeman outside
the window of Lewis and Allenby. In *The Dark Girl
Dress'd in Blue*, did we but know it, it is an affair of a mis-
understanding and a five-pound note. What we witness is
their casual meeting before it ripens to a momentary friend-
ship. In another breath the blue delphinium will turn on
the wind of chance and the huge blue bell-flower dangle and
sway before him upon the pavement. But what does it
mean that, at the young man's feet, the words, "Try Harper's
Soap Powder ", and in the other direction, upside down as
we look at it, the word " Bootrees ", spelt thus, are chalked
upon the paving stone ? Is this an advertisement ? For it
cannot be by chance that the young man in the riding
boots is standing on this particular paving stone. It must be
a mystery till we see the answer : *I'm the Dark Girl Dressed
in Blue*.

It comes a few steps further along the pavement, and
again it is this afternoon, or tomorrow, or next week, for
it does not matter, this is August in London. What we
behold is a young woman, *The Dark Girl Dressed in Blue*,
standing in a shop door, and holding by its edges, in both
hands, the borrowed five-pound note. That special paper
and scrolled lettering are known the world over, but she
holds it up that passers-by may read the number on the
bank note. Let us forget the incident, however ! For what
we behold is a fantastic figure in an appropriate, but most
extraordinary setting. She is dressed in full mantle and crinoline which cover her entirely, from neck to ground. In fact,
her crinoline begins, not from her waist, but from her chin.
She wears a high bonnet with artificial flowers in the brim,
and it is tied with ribbons beneath her chin and at the level
of her cheeks. Then we see her white cuffs and her pale-blue

gloves that hold up the five-pound note to passers-by. Except for that, she is altogether hidden in the monstrous cage, and it is a cage without bars. The diameter of the crinoline at its base is exactly equal to its height from foot to chin. Her shape, therefore, is that of an isosceles triangle, at the apex of which we see her face and bonnet. We have the feeling that we could unwrap this monstrous parcel after untying the ribbons at her throat, for the wide ends of the ribbon float loose upon her bosom just above her hands, that hold the five-pound note. The crinoline, itself, is covered by an immense over-skirt descending to half-way below her hidden knees, while over that again she wears the mantle. A ghost of the mantle and crinoline we may all have seen in the back streets of our cities and provincial towns, where some old pensioner, all in black, plays the diminished spectre of what has come down in the world from the Champs-Élysées to Laburnum Road, and along to the Poor House and Infirmary. What we never thought to behold is a young woman in bonnet and mantle, wearing this nun-like concealment for the elderly. There are so many sorts of crinolines. Crinolines for the ballroom, or looped up for walking. Crinolines that are worn in carriages, where two ladies sit, side by side, parasol in hand, their billowing skirts filling the whole body of their fantastically light and elegant vehicle, and we would bargain our souls away in order to hear the fabulous inanities of their conversation.

But we will not leave the pavement of Regent Street for the carriages of the Avenue du Bois and Champs-Élysées. Instead, we wonder how *The Dark Girl Dressed in Blue* moved into position in the doorway. Did she glide, like a pyramid, in and out among the other cones of shadow? For she is the shape of a yew pyramid, of an obelisk of box or yew. Like a person in a machine, at the centre of a complex structure ; and she is standing, in fact, most appropriately, in the doorway of the Magasin des Modes, as we see it written under the window, where the latest crinolines are exposed for sale. A label says, " BEST STEEL ", and behind it we see the dummy crinoline and a blank space above it, and then, supported on a rod, the smaller steel hoops that underlie the bodice. To the right of that, the enormous substructure of a crinoline hangs, sideways, in the window ; while, hung from the ceiling, the hoops of another crinoline dangle like a cage. An advertisement reads : " CRINOLINES STAYS OUTFITS FOR ABROAD ", and even, " CRINOLINES FOR CHILDREN ". The other window has the same aerial crinolines floating, hung up like cages, or like fishing nets ; and more remarkable, another dummy with, at the foot of it, an opening like the door in a dog-kennel for convenience of the feet in walking. Through the curtained doorway we see the interior of the Magasin des Modes, and a glimpse of a shop assistant standing at the counter ; while over the head of *The Dark Girl Dressed in Blue* as she waits in the door, a huge scarlet crinoline is suspended and we see what otherwise we should have no chance of seeing, the ribbed interior of a crinoline. It floats over the head of *The Dark Girl Dressed in Blue* like one of the opened umbrellas in a general store in some out-of-the-way village, or down in the slums. So much so, that the true purpose of those ribs and hoops only dawns on us when we look again at the living person in the doorway who wears a crinoline. The floating skeleton even touches another that is hung up by its side. We could wish it were possible to catch a reflection of her figure, in its setting, not in a mirror or the glass window at her side, but upside down, in a pool of water, so that the reflection joined itself immediately to the reality and we could see the skeletons of crinolines in their bare bones, together with the embryo or chrysalis of the crinoline, and then that immense hoop inhabited and put to purpose. It is a travesty surrounded on all sides by the fantastic and improbable. We would imagine, for ourselves, *The Dark Girl Dressed in Blue* lying in the grass under the darkening trees of August, or on a sofa under the cut crystal of some prodigious chandelier. For the hoops are some five feet in circumference. They would sag and lie flat under her body, but the frilled interior of this immense flower would not otherwise lose its shape. The corolla of the giant fuchsia has only fallen and is lying on its side. The stamens emerge out of the blossom, and have grown longer than the flower. They protrude and dangle. We see the long, laced bootees or slippers of *The Dark Girl Dressed in Blue* and, so doing, have known the point and beauty of the crinoline.

And suddenly, coming down to Piccadilly Circus, the sky over Whitehall and to the east, towards the City and St Paul's, becomes the sea sky of chalk cliffs and of the salt tides. It is the alternative London to Hampstead and to the Surrey hills. Seagulls, in their hundreds, feed on the muddy shores. The first oysters have come in baskets to the oyster bars. We feel a touch of autumn in the shadows of high buildings. The white clouds over London are not pagan statues as in the skies of Italy and Greece ; not gods and goddesses drawn in chariots by white horses. They are the white sails of sailing ships. A sea wind blows into London. And it brings us, in imagination, the long line of smoke of a vessel low on the horizon, far out to sea. Seen, this is curious, from across the street and but a foot or two above the cast-iron seaside railing. Now, at the end of summer, we have this vision of a stroll along the sea front. We are " Off to Brighton ", if only for the moment.

We are passing under a red-and-white striped awning. The heavy lamp of a public house projects out and above this, and on the far side of the road there is the open sea.

We are so near to everything that we see nothing but the outer line of the building immediately in front, and not a door or window. The perspective of Brighton is that few inches of blank wall. It is because the drama is in the persons. The first thing we see is the tail of a dog, and its shadow on the paving stone. That shadow, even, is a proof that we are among the living. There follows a blank space and they are upon us.

The whole width of the pavement is taken up by them. A father and his pair of daughters bear down on us. He walks with a daughter on either arm. The movement is from his pointed trousers and their billowing skirts. He has square-ended shoes, and not only his trousers but his entire suit are peculiar in cut and colour. It is a light blue cloth with red lines woven into it ; and the trousers, which are full-waisted, and have no crease, narrow or taper in most extravagant fashion at his ankles. His coat is only fastened by one button at his neck, and has a collar of black braid or velvet, and a black edging down both its faces, while, under that opening, we see his waistcoat, with no wings but cut level on the straight. These two details seem to give his character and dictate his walk. For he comes towards us with a daughter on each arm, holding in his gloved right hand his walking stick, which has a carved bone handle of the sort we know from stick-racks in old country houses. This walking automaton wears a low collar and a red stock with a heavy tie-pin. He bears down on us with those curious limbs and pointed shoes, his legs and arms, alike, cut full, like Turkish trousers, and his gloved left hand protruding, like the hand of an automaton, from his sleeve. For, above that, his face and eyeglass with string tied to his coat button are quite impassive and he walks as though sightless, guided at each arm.

The head of this peculiar being is a thing apart which

could be lifted out of its collar and put under a glass shade. His left eye, without the monocle, has a cold stare. But the character of the head, the cord and monocle apart, comes from his black moustache which flows into and mingles with his whiskers. Those are long and jagged, like lightning in a miniature storm between a pair of Leyden jars. They flow from ear to cheekbone, and nearly touch his shoulders. His ears we cannot see ; but his hair is brushed out again above them, at the level of his eyebrows, while his hat is the most fantastic, yet appropriate feature. For it is a low, blue bowler hat, of the same colour as his suit, with a black band, but so shallow a dome that it is not higher than a straw hat, moreover it has no brim to speak of, and nothing but a thin edge by which to take it in the hand, like a ' deer-stalker ' made solid but light blue.

Now we come to his daughters on each arm. One is dark, and the other fair. They are seventeen or nineteen years old ; and both are pretty, and must be the belles of the apartments where they stay. The dark girl wears a tartan dress and crinoline of red and white, with a black shawl. Her bodice fastens beautifully with a white collar ; and there is a lovely passage or episode with her white sleeve, her gloved hand, and the light-blue parasol that she holds behind her head. She wears a low-crowned black hat with red and white feathers. Her sister wears a light-green dress and crinoline with three black circles at its hem and four black dots, like buttons, down its front. Her bodice fastens as charmingly ; she has a low-crowned black hat with a black pompom and white feather, while from her white shawl, which has touches of light blue in it, her sleeve and gloved hand hold up a rose-pink parasol, but in the air, coquettishly, and not to frame her head. We see nothing of the feet of either girl. They are quite hidden in their crinolines.

OFF TO BRIGHTON.

At their side an old gentleman in a yellow bath chair is pushed, painfully, along the gutter. At his back we see his footman's corded top hat and cockade. But he is overwhelmed by street musicians. Four street urchins, in enormous caps, and long frock coats and long, untidy hair are in the way of everyone. A little boy blows his trumpet right in the old man's ear ; another, in a green frock coat, lifts his cap to beg from passers-by ; while a third child, driven out of the gutter by the bath chair, hugs his brass instrument, which is almost bigger than himself ; and his companion, facing the street, blows a kind of clarionet, hopefully, in the direction of a young girl who is driving by, and away from us, in a pony chaise. It is a light wicker carriage. She holds the reins, and an elderly person, her mother or governess, sits by her side. A white pony draws the pony chaise ; while the young girl, who is very pretty, whip in one hand and reins in the other, is dressed in white with a black hat, and has a pale-blue rug or carriage wrap over her knees.

What else do we see ? In the distance the chain pier, and a man with a telescope looking out to sea. Three or four ladies on horseback, the long skirts of the Amazons trailing nearly to the ground ; a man in the green Volunteer uniform of 1859 riding a donkey ; many persons in top hats, along the pavement ; and a carriage drawn by a pair of horses with a coachman on the box. But our glances wander away towards the sea. The sky is white with seagulls' wings. The back view of two ladies, one in red and one in yellow, with their flat, black hats and netted chignons, yields us the silhouette or outline of the hour, for they walk as women have never walked before or since, a character which comes from their crinolines and the shawls worn low upon their shoulders. Leaning on the railing immediately beside them are a pair of boatmen or fishermen in oilskin hats, seaboots, and enormous, baggy oilskin breeches. They could only be boatmen or fishermen from the way they stand. Nearer to us, there is a little family scene. A small boy, to one side of his mother's red crinoline, looks hesitatingly towards a ragged child, who touches his cap, and leads an empty goat carriage. It is a little carriage, painted a light blue, with seats for two children facing each other, and we wonder what could be more fantastic or improbable than this goat car led by a slum child, close to the crinoline, beside the sea. At Brighton, and at Folkestone, there are, then, the footprints of satyrs upon the sands. We wonder where the goat is stabled ; remembering from our own childhood the patter of his hooves upon the asphalt, and the little and curious jangle of the goat carriage upon the Leas. But, there, it is along the cliff. Here, it is low and flat, and only a foot or two above the sea.

But our trip to Brighton leads back, with no more ado, to London. We hear, in imagination, the noise of the train crossing the iron girders and rolling in to London, over the Thames, to Charing Cross. We are five minutes' walk from Regent Street and Piccadilly. To Trafalgar Square and up the Haymarket, near to where we started on our walk upon another, or the self-same afternoon. It does not matter. *The Bond Street Beau* will be upon his West End beat. We would go this afternoon by side streets past the music publishers. We are passing Mitzler's in Great Marlborough Street, and pause to look in his shop window. It is stacked from floor to ceiling with the latest song covers, and in the centre there is a special feature of a quadrille on popular tunes by C. Godfrey junior, which is the new hit. Copies of this are stuck in long lines upon the window and are arranged at every angle upon a table. But it is not the music but the illustrated song cover that attracts us, not because it is a particularly good specimen, but for the reason

26

that it represents a pianist thumping out the quadrille upon a piano, from the top of which cascades of song covers descend on both sides of him and are heaped upon the floor. The pianist, who is of the sort that is hired to play at dances, wears a blue tail coat with brass buttons, yellow nankeen trousers, and red slippers. He sits with his back to us on a hideous music stool ; his hair from front to back is parted in the centre ; and with hair and coat tails flying and slippers nearly kicking off his feet he thumps out *The Great Sensation*.

The song covers cascading down, some of them littering the top of the upright piano, and others in mid-air, or lying on the ground, are all the latest hits. We see among them *The Dundreary Galop*, with Edward Sothern the creator of that character, not, as usual, with arms stretched, yawning in a chair, but standing upright in a padded dressing-gown ; [1] an abbreviated or shorthand version, as it were, of *Off to Brighton* ; and in a corner a copy in miniature of the very cover we are looking at. Falling down, full tilt, and half-way to the floor, is a song cover which the artist has elongated to its full length as though it interested him more than all the others. This is *The Perfect Cure*, by J. H. Stead, drawn in the curious costume in which he sang that famous song. He is a red-and-white striped Pierrot, without the long, flopping sleeves of Pierrot, but with his arms held straight down at his sides, in the posture, precisely, of *Le Grand Gilles* of Watteau. But there is, as we shall see, a particular reason for this attitude.

The Perfect Cure wears a tall white dunce's cap with a red

[1] The rôle of Lord Dundreary played by Edward Sothern (1836–1881) was in the play *Our American Cousin*. The part as originally written when the piece was produced in New York consisted of about twenty lines. Sothern expanded and performed the part a thousand times in America, and then brought the play to England, where he appeared at the Haymarket, November 11th, 1861.

band round his head, his face is powdered white like Pierrot, but he has a moustache and little imperial, and his striped suit of red and white, in vertical lines, is completed by a white tie like a ruff, white socks, and red dancing shoes. This song *The Perfect Cure* was, originally, an air *The Monkey and the Nuts*, written by Blewitt, who had been musical director of Vauxhall Gardens and was a prolific composer for the pantomimes at the Olympic, Drury Lane, and Covent Garden. After the chorus, J. H. Stead bounced up and down rigidly to the dance music, it being computed that, about 1861, when the song was such a rage at Weston's Music Hall, he must have frequently jumped some four hundred and fifty times in the course of an evening, continuing this for upwards of a year. In fact we see him, thanks to the artist's convention, in mid-air, bouncing rigidly with his hands to his sides, and can realize how the height of his leap is helped and exaggerated by those long stripes of red and white. We will let this red-and-white Pierrot be our introduction to the pleasures of tonight, when we will walk the streets upon an August night in London.

All the covers shown so cleverly in this music cover for the *Quadrille* by C. Godfrey junior are by the same artist, and if we lean forward into the shop window we shall read his signature. Not only upon this example, which he has made, so to speak, into a quadrille of his own song covers, but, also, on many other music covers here and there in Mitzler's window. He must be the artist most in request for these coloured lithographs, the few best specimens of which, from many hundreds or even thousands, are our inspiration for these present pages. One of the most unequal of artists, as we shall see, for while many, if not the majority, of his plates are mere hack work and very poor indeed, he is, at rare moments and for no apparent reason, not inferior

to Constantin Guys and the supreme artist of so brief an
hour that he could be called, with no exaggeration, the
delineator of morning, noon and night in London.

Alfred Concanen is the name of this forgotten artist,
ignored by all save those few amateurs who are lovers of
the old music halls, and omitted altogether from the dictionaries of painters. He was an Irishman, belonging to an
old Anglo-Irish family from Co. Galway which has produced
more than one famous member of the legal profession, but
the family, as a whole, were probably ashamed of the
adventurous, perhaps bibulous scion of their stock who
haunted the music halls and went round doing hack work
for the song publishers. He was born in London in 1835,
and seems to have passed most of his life there. It is
unlikely that Concanen learned drawing as a student, for
this could only lead him by aberration to the music halls.
We would think it more probable that this Irishman had
ambitions, himself, as a singer and vocalist, and as well,
a ready-made talent for drawing and for caricature. Failure
in the one direction would then lead him easily and im-
perceptibly into the other. In this manner we would explain
how he came to do song covers for the music publishers.

There are early examples of song covers by George
Cruikshank and by Robert Seymour, steel engravings which
are no different from book illustrations, but by the late
'fifties lithography had superseded steel engraving and song
covers had become coloured lithographs. For some reason,
while aquatint and woodcut, in their respective periods,
have been carefully studied, lithography has been neglected
or ignored, probably because of the immensity and un-
wieldiness of the subject and because of the stigma still
attaching to chromolithography as a term. That is to say,
aquatint has been studied exhaustively by Miss Prideaux
and by others, and several books have been devoted to the

woodcut illustrators of the 'sixties, but next to nothing has been written on lithography. It is an art which includes the beautiful portraits by Brandard and by Bouvier of the dancers of the Romantic Ballet, the Eastern landscapes of Sir David Wilkie, the Spanish and Oriental scenes and figures of J. F. Lewis, and the bird books of John Gould. Brandard, we may note, is the master of the ballet music cover, a specialized art form which flourished in the 'forties. Some ten years later, lithography was used for the song covers from the music halls, and from about 1859 Concanen becomes the supreme exponent of the art. His golden period is in or about 1862 or 1863, at the period, exactly, when Sothern was appearing at the Haymarket in the part of Lord Dundreary. This was the epoch, too, of the *lion comique* ; of the Great Vance, and of George Leybourne or " Champagne Charlie ". But this is not a history of the London music halls. Our interest in music-hall song covers lies neither in the words nor music. Our subject is Concanen ; and only Concanen now and then. Nine times out of ten they are but song covers, and nothing more.

Why is Concanen so good occasionally ; and at all other times so bad ? We are to imagine that he was paid a uniform price, probably two guineas, for his song covers. At certain periods, working for different music publishers, he may have produced nearly a hundred song covers in a year. A great many of them, particularly in later years, are but the comedian's portrait redrawn from a photograph. Many more are but the full-length figure of the actor, in character. But with no background. Even so, some are remarkable as portraits of comedians, and their total fills a complete gallery of types of humour. But his more important music covers are altogether exceptional, while, technically, they are among the most beautiful lithographs ever executed.

What was the occasion for their sudden and mysterious excellence ? There could be three reasons : that the comedian was appearing in a new song and was spending his money in advertisement ; that Concanen, himself, felt inspired and liked the opportunity ; or that the firm of lithographers needed a show piece to draw attention to their skill. Concanen was, at times, his own lithographer and made his own drawing on the stone. He alone, for instance, drew and lithographed *The Bond Street Beau*. His signature, only, is upon *What Our Swells Are Coming To !*, one of his finest drawings, which we have not yet described. On the other hand, the signature Concanen and Lee appears upon *Kleptomania, Off to Brighton*, and *The Dark Girl Dress'd in Blue*. Lee, in such cases, would be lithographer ; while another signature, Concanen & Siebe, is to be seen upon *The Hansom Galop*, one of his transcendental music covers, as a drawing and as a coloured lithograph. Credit, then, must be divided in many instances between the draughtsman and the lithographer ; while, over the actual process of lithography, more than one craftsman was probably employed. The master lithographer would sketch out the drawing upon the stone, and another would fill in the details, the hands and faces, or the background. Perhaps a different craftsman attended to the colouring. It is a case of composite credit. A firm of lithographers could make a good lithograph from a weak and indifferent drawing. Is the credit for the completed lithograph as a work of art to be given to the artist who made the sketch, or to the firm of lithographers who printed it ?

This is not so simple a question as that of mezzotint or line engraving. Prints taken from the portraits of Reynolds and Gainsborough, or the French engravings of the eighteenth century, bear the signature of some well-known engraver. This is the case, too, with the English sporting aquatints of the early nineteenth century. But the music covers of the 'sixties are instances of commercial lithography. However, as on occasion Concanen was his own lithographer, and in the result his music covers are in no way inferior to those that carry the signature of a firm of professional lithographers, we call his music covers ' Concanens ', and do not differentiate, where that applies, between the various firms who printed them. Otherwise the attributions are too complicated. Where Concanen has not made his own lithograph, his peculiar genius and aptitude has inspired his printers. The true parallel to this situation is in the case of the Japanese woodcuts, where, for instance, Hokusai or Utamaro take all the credit ; yet the cutting and printing of the woodblocks was done, almost invariably, by firms of craftsmen. But the pair of Japanese artists in question were fully capable of such achievement and did, on occasion, cut their own blocks and do their own printing. Their woodcuts, as a whole, are Hokusai and Utamaro ; and by the same authority, Concanen must remain Concanen, whether printed by himself, or by one or other of the firms for whom he worked.

But there is now the method of Concanen to be considered, and this falls of itself into many different headings. In order to illustrate our meaning we will quote a stanza or two of doggerel from the song *Did You Ever, No I Never* :

Did you ever see policemen
  Carry parasols ?
Or the judges on the bench
  Nursing penny dolls ?
Did you ever know a Welshman,
  Who was not named Jones ?
Did you ever eat red herrings,
  That were destitute of bones ?

CHORUS

Did you ever, ever know
　Things so very rum ?
No I never, never did
　Since in the world I've come.

Did you ever don a suit
　Of feathers stuck in tar ?
Or ever dance the Highland fling
　Upon a tramway car ?
Did you ever wear your socks
　Above your Blucher boots ?
Or walk about with your shirt outside
　Of your ordinary suits ?

For this song cover, which is deficient or even very poor indeed in colour, Concanen, whose signature alone appears, has worked upon an arbitrary plan, choosing only to illustrate those queries from the song that he could fit into his argument. Upon the left and right sides, respectively, of the cover there are incidents drawn from two couplets that we have not quoted in our abbreviated version of the song.

Did you ever know a cabman
　Who could never curse ?

·　　·　　·　　·

Or a cripple with two wooden legs
　A skating round a rink ?

The cabby, with a pleasant smile, is arguing on the pavement with an old gentleman, wearing a frilled shirt and carrying an umbrella, but who is the creation of Concanen, that is to say, he is not mentioned in the song. Upon the other side, at the door of a public house, with " Welsh Ales " upon the window, and the name of the publican, Jones, written large at the corner under the inn sign of *The Golden Leek*, we see the " cripple with two wooden legs ", but carrying his skates in his hand and not " A skating round a rink ". Two half-truths, then, for this illustrates :

> Did you ever know a Welshman
> Who was not named Jones ?

but by symbol, and without the Welshman, and gives us in the same breath the cripple with two wooden legs, and his skates, but not the skating rink.

The foreground is taken up by four policemen, walking one behind another, carrying parasols ; but there is no allusion to red herrings, or to judges sitting on the bench. Neither is there any reference to the suit of feathers stuck in tar ; though, on the back of an omnibus which advertises " Coote's Messenger of Love Waltz — Great Success of the Season " (C. Coote Junior being composer of *Did You Ever, No I Never*) we see a man in kilt and sporran dancing the Highland fling among the other passengers upon the top of the tramway car ; while, as for illustration of :

> Did you ever wear your socks
> Above your Blucher boots ?

we find that the whole clue and centre to the drawing comes from the comedian himself, who illustrates, at one and the same time, both the couplet just quoted and as well :

> Or walk about with your shirt outside
> Of your ordinary suits ?

He wears a top hat, carries a neatly rolled and incongruous umbrella, and his ' ordinary ' trousers disappear into his socks which are pulled up over and above his Blucher boots, Bluchers, be it remembered, being smaller than, or indeed half the height of, Wellingtons. His shirt, most emphatically, is outside his suit, a shirt which is elaborate and old-fashioned to our eyes, with hemmed sleeves and enormous cuffs, and an arrangement down the front for fastening the lining of the waistcoat. Again, like the red-and-white striped Pierrot of *The Perfect Cure*, his arms and hands are straight down at his sides, and what reveals him as the comedian is the assurance in his eccentricity, his confident walk, and the monocle screwed into his left eye. His white shirt, white socks, and pallid face are as conspicuous as the ' living statues ' of the old music halls, who were painted white from head to foot. He is the embodiment of inanity, with his top hat and high collar, his umbrella and cravat. Two other buildings mentioned in the song, a bank and the Aquarium, are in the background across the crowded street. The bank has that word written above it, while the Aquarium is a typical aquarium with a glass roof. But seven other incidents in the song, each referred to in its own couplet, make no appearance at all and are omitted from the music cover. Thus, of a total of twenty episodes or couplets in the song, ten in all are illustrated, and two of these are combined into the one figure of the comedian or dude.

What is of importance in *Did You Ever, No I Never* is that Concanen has taken the comedian out of the theatre into the street. The song, according to the inscription upon the cover, was " Sung by all the Leading Comedians " ; are we to imagine, in the rôle and costume shown upon the cover, or is this the artist's invention ? The comedian, after all, could come on, alternatively, in a suit of tar and feathers, as about to dance a Highland fling ; as a Welshman ; a cabby who never swore ; or a policeman carrying a parasol. Or he could appear as a judge nursing a penny doll ; or a person carrying a huge and boneless red herring. Otherwise he might come on in the clothes he always wore to sing his song ; or wearing something special and peculiar for the occasion.

This brings us to the different types of presentment practised by Concanen, for *Did You Ever, No I Never*, incidentally but a poor example of his talents, is only interesting as showing several of the forms in combination. It is a simultaneous presentment of ten episodes, two of them, as we have seen, combined in the person of the singer of the song. But three of these, the bank, the Aquarium, and the Welshman Jones, are illustrated by the simple expedient of writing their names upon the outsides of the appropriate buildings, a device of but little more value than the slogans of the Fascist party stencilled upon Italian walls. The comedian appears as a living person among the fictions of his song. He is, even, more alive because more conspicuous than they. He, at least, appears as living flesh and bone before us upon the stage. The others are but joking questions: *Did You Ever, No I Never*. They pass as quickly as images before the brain, at intervals of a few seconds as he sings his song. And their whole point is that they are unreal, as evidenced by the song title. They are ridiculous and preposterous and make no sense : being mere contradictions and conundrums.

The music covers, taken as a whole, vary from pure illustration to mere fantasy. *Off to Brighton* is the imaginary scene presented, not in its typical buildings, but in its persons. Not a sign of the stucco houses or bow windows of Brighton. The architectural scene, regarded as theatre, as a painted wing, consists of no more than a vertical line, a red-and-white striped awning, and the projecting gas lamp of a public house on which is painted " Brighton Tipper Ales ". But we are down at Brighton for a breath of sea air and this is expressed in the walk of the automaton father and his pair of daughters, for they are promenading as if along the pier. That, again, is as though upon a stage, except that the boards run the other way. The crowd moves in three directions, or at least they move in two directions, and are stationary, for the children's brass band is playing in the gutter, while the charming young girl in the blue-and-white dress drives past and away from us in her pony chaise. How high does *Off to Brighton* rank as a drawing? We would answer that this not more than moderate specimen of Concanen is as good as a drawing by John Leech. It compares with the large sea-side woodcuts of Scarborough done for the *Illustrated London News*, of which the Scarborough Sands is the best example, with the local jockey carriages driving far out at the margin of the waves, while the foreground is occupied by ladies in hooped skirts and hirsute gentlemen in the loose, flopping check suits that were the fashion, with a Skye terrier like a weeping willow in the centre that, in commentary, is the complete epitome of that peculiar time.[1] Concanen is as good as that; but we shall see that he can be better.

Off to Brighton, we observe, is of another type from *Did You Ever, No I Never* because its personalities are imaginary. They are not drawn from the words of the song, for, in fact, *Off to Brighton* has no words. It is a dance tune or quadrille. But, in the midst of *Did You Ever, No I Never* we see the comedian or comic singer moving in the crowd. It is not, though, necessarily his portrait. But his pallid appearance, as though the limelight is upon him, picks him out, and he is given such unreality or improbability compared with the other figures that his identity is certain. In yet another type of music cover, that of *The Dark Girl Dress'd in Blue*, Harry Clifton and Kate Harley, the protagonists, are drawn and presented to us as portraits and in costume, but not before their backcloth. They are shown in actual life, with a policeman, hansom cabs, and omnibuses in the

[1] " Part of Scarborough ", drawn by John Leech in the *Illustrated London News* for 26 September, 1857.

foreground, and behind, the Exhibition building of 1862 flying the flags of all the nations. *The Bond Street Beau* may appear on the pavement of Bond Street, or before his painted backcloth that is Bond Street, all the same, and even that particular section of it with such and such a shop or building, or the well-known Bond Street corner. *Kleptomania*, again, is pure invention. In the words of that song there is to be found no mention, none whatever, of Lewis and Allenby, or even of Bond Street. Was it sung by Frank Hall before a curtain with the entrance to Lewis and Allenby painted upon it ? This would seem unlikely. Is the gentleman involved in the incident, who wears a blue tail coat and grey top hat, a portrait of Frank Hall ? This, too, would seem improbable. We believe that the characters in *Kleptomania*, like the incident, are imaginary. There is no allusion to the two young women in the doggerel verses. Yet we trace one of the heroines, and recognize her, in *The Dark Girl Dress'd in Blue*. And she appears again, of course, in the answer, *I'm the Dark Girl Dressed in Blue*, " sung by Kate Harley ".

In another type of music cover Concanen depicts the comedian or vocalist, in person, against a typical background suggested by his song. The scene, therefore, is general and not particular, as in *The Bond Street Beau*. But the huge gamut of the old music hall, with glittering pantomime for winter, presents other figures than the dude and droll. For the *lion comique* and *The Perfect Cure*, near descendants of the poetical *Grand Gilles* of Watteau, may be billed in the same programme as the Nigger Minstrels. There may be many of us who remember, as I do, the black-faced comedians of the sands. They are even, or were till lately, to be seen dancing in the streets of London, more often to the theatre queues. Here, then, is their original or prototype. This is one of the most delicate in colour of all the music covers. It is a scene somewhere in the suburbs, where the town becomes the country, but remember that this is an early Concanen and we are writing of long ago. He is, therefore, probably with a little professional assistance, his own lithographer.

E. W. Mackney, the Negro Delineator, stands before us in the middle of the road. It is a summer day. The trees are in leaf. We see them, and a church spire, above a low brick wall. The tone of the whole drawing is in pink and red, and pearly grey and white. Polly Crow wears white trousers or pantaloons with a thick red stripe, trousers which end high above his ankles in 'plantation' style to show his shoes that are too big for him and his untied and flapping shoe laces. It is the negro tradition, like his tattered long tail coat which will not button across his chest and leaves his white shirt front open. This is the finery of the negro king, to be completed by a battered top hat and umbrella. The tail coat, we are to presume, has been stolen or bartered from a missionary, but it has been embellished with a few white spots or circles to mark the negro minstrel; and he wears, not a top hat, but a crumpled white paper hat which is like a top hat, but without a brim. The nigger minstrel is inherent in the striped trousers and white cotton shirt.

But the true rôle of Polly Crow lies in his banjo and his blackened face. The banjo is beautifully drawn, its flat disk being of an ivory tint, which, with his black hand upon it, twanging at the strings, makes a passage reminiscent of the ivories and sepia blacks in Hokusai, but we are thinking not of his prints, but of his rare books enriched with mica and silver, with sprinkled gold dust and metallic colours. The long handle of the banjo is held, in minstrel fashion, in Polly Crow's left hand. It lies against the distant church spire, and we can follow its wires across his body as with the comedians of Callot and of Watteau.

But the music is different. For the strings are metal wires, and had he a partner he would hit a tambourine or play the bones. The nigger minstrel, according to convention, had a stand-up collar and a big white tie, this being, of course, in order to accentuate the blackness of his face. This first and greatest of black-faced comedians has an enormous white bow tie, one wing of which touches on his banjo, while his collar is that of Lord Byron or the Beaux of the Regency come down to the cotton plantations and the black savannah. His face, above that collar and below his paper hat, is most sensitively drawn and a beautiful portrayal of a person singing. This is not the black mask of Mezzetin, but a good-looking young man with his face blacked. We see from his red lips that he is no negro, that he has not exchanged Niger or Congo for the Mississippi. His eyes are rolling, that is to say, we see the whites of his eyes, but it is because he is aware of an audience behind his back.

He is singing or serenading for the benefit of a young woman who comes out of the grocer's shop into the street. For we only see one side of the road. We are the invisible audience, but the far side is a living backcloth. It is a little grocer's shop standing at the corner, with old-fashioned square panes and many objects in the shop window. The low brick wall runs from the shop front into the distance, off the scene, and at its edge, close to another of the old street posts that are so typical of Concanen that they could be taken for his signature, we see an old lady and gentleman walking away, he wearing gaiters and a curious low-crowned top hat, and she presenting to us the typical silhouette of the eighteen-forties with a coal-scuttle bonnet. This pair of figures, who are not unlike Bakst's Philistines for Schumann's *Carnaval*, betray the early epoch of this particular music cover. For it is one of the first works of

Concanen and may date from 1858 or 1859. But we return to the shop front ; to the birdcage and pots of flowers upon the first-floor window-ledges, and to the advertisements that are displayed in the shop window. To the fat old shopkeeper in the door, talking to a child ; but, more than all else, to the charming young girl who has just this moment stepped out from the shop on to the street. The shop-keeper is still looking in her direction, and we seem to hear the noise of her feet upon the pavement. She has a dog upon a lead, and this little detail, if nothing else, would draw our attention to her short, looped-up skirt and very pretty feet.

The accent of this delightful drawing is upon good looks and youth, for the old couple turn their backs and walk away. It is upon the young street singer, who sang in the music halls but never in the streets, and upon the young and fascinating girl whom Concanen has made death-less, for a mere moment of her day, for a mere instant in her daily shopping. She wears a pert and brimless white bowler hat, for it has that shape, upon her glossy hair, has long earrings, and a full-sleeved coat or jacket, of hip length, and in a mulberry or purple colour. From the edge of this we see her gloved hand that holds the lead. With her other arm she holds her parcels. Her bell-shaped skirt or crinoline is lavender or pearly grey, crisscrossed or hatched with white, which gives the effect of a starched cotton. It is looped up, not far below her knees, in wide flounces that show the level circumference of her petticoat or under-skirt. The enticing profile of this young woman, against a window-pane, under the provocative slant of her white bowler hat, is continued by her full sleeve that gives pro-minence to her long wrist, and down the lead, to her crinoline and long calf-length boots. These boots are particularly delightful because they accentuate her lightness, under that

41

airy crinoline, and make her walk like a dancer in a ballet skirt. She comes down out of the grocer's shop and picks her steps. The old couple walking away and never looking back, and the fat old shopkeeper whose glance follows her, narrows down the drama to two persons, the young woman and the street singer.

How essentially English, and of our race, is this work of art by an ignored master ! It is not only because of a superficial resemblance, owing to the importance in this drawing of a red brick wall, that we are reminded of *The Cherry Barrow*, *The Ballad Seller*, and other paintings by Henry Walton, one of the most exquisite of our eighteenth-century artists. Those readers who know *The Cherry Barrow*, in its original, or from the well-known mezzotint, will concur that it is the physical serenity of the young woman standing by the fruit stall in her simple dress and tall bearskin hat, for it has that form and appears to be fashioned of that material, which is far more important, aesthetically, than the very ordinary subject of the painting. For the rest, besides the pretty children, it is a brick wall and a high London building. *The Ballad Seller*, too, is but a young woman buying street ballads, the vendor of the ballads, and a stretch of wall. But the tone of this Victorian music cover reminds us of the colour of Henry Walton. Walton is a London painter, as much as Lavreince or Baudouin are Parisian in their gouache drawings. It is the same with Concanen. With Concanen, the Irishman, it is always London and no other city. Even when we follow him to Brighton, it is only to meet Londoners who have come down for a few days for a breath of air.

We could be in Hampstead, or Highgate, or Stoke Newington. It is an early nineteenth-century grocer's shop. Or it could be in Kilburn, or Islington, or even Paddington. In some old suburb with its own High Street, within sound of the great bell of St Paul's. Where the red glare over great London lights the sky, and the million wheels of her ceaseless traffic can be heard ; but where the owl yet hoots on frosty nights and the red robin leaps upon the wintry bough. Three or four miles, not more, from Piccadilly. For there were such suburbs, in the middle of the nineteenth century. Within reach of the music halls, within the beat of the street cries and street singers. The young woman, of course, is someone's daughter, and well known in the grocer's shop. It is more than likely that they have known her since she was a child ; that they have watched her growing into a young and pretty woman. How her short hooped skirt and soft leather boots contrast with the red-and-white striped trousers and tattered coat tails of this first of Nigger Minstrels ! And again, how the ragged clothes of this serenader, playing his banjo, are in contradiction to his smooth black face ! Chirgwin, the " White-Eyed Kaffir ", whom many may remember, was a comedian of quite another import and conception. So closely was he modelled upon the negro coon with his thin limbs and the gestures of his black hands, that it was necessary for him to wear a white steeple hat and have a white patch or lozenge over one eye in order to confirm that it was pretence and that he was black-faced and not black-skinned. Chirgwin could, and doubtless did, sing upon seaside piers, one among many chocolate-faced coons, but it was impossible to imagine any other setting for him. It would have been a travesty to depict Chirgwin, banjo in hand, singing in the street. Particularly in the half-rural peacefulness of this small suburb. I have heard Chirgwin myself, and my instinct tells me that he could never have serenaded this young woman. For his own merits, Chirgwin was inadmissible in a work of art, whereas Mackney, his forerunner and predecessor, the Negro Delineator or Nigger Minstrel, could be drawn by the most delicate and fastidious of painters.

We have written at length of this beautiful lithograph because it represents Concanen in a vein which every reader will admire and understand. This obscure draughtsman, who is unknown to the dictionaries of painters, who is not even mentioned in the histories of art, and whose only audience is among the lovers of old music halls, here achieves one of the works of art of the decade. It would be tedious to compare him with Rossetti and the Pre-Raphaelites, only to prove that in this one example out of many he is alive, and they are dead. Pinwell, Boyd Houghton, Frederick Sandys, draughtsmen who made drawings for the woodcuts of the 'sixties, how dead and archaic they are, too, beside this living master. But only, as we must know, the master of a flying moment, never to come again. Because circumstances were not propitious ; because of a deterioration in his subject and the decay of genius in the music halls ? We cannot tell. It is more probable that the secret lay with the lithographers. The later series of music covers that is illustrated with portraits drawn from photographs gives us the clue. Such was the degradation of his talent, and being an Irishman from Co. Galway it is not improbable that disappointment drove him to drink.

The very short period, extending over two or three years at most, during which Concanen produced his finest prints, whether by his own hand alone or aided by the commercial lithographers, must now be considered both in relation to other great artists of the theatre and with regard to the choice of the particular artist to whom he most nearly corresponds. There is no parallel, it is obvious, between his peculiar calling, that of a draughtsman for popular song covers, and the elaborate set scenes from comedies of Zoffany and de Wilde. Those are of the school of Hogarth ; they

are conversation pieces with appropriate action upon the
scene; and if we add to them the delightful gouache paintings
from Dutch comedies by Cornelis Troost we have one
aspect, only, of the theatre. The pictures by the Dutchman
are more interesting because of the artificiality of the cos-
tumes and canals, and for their echoes of Italian comedy and
the acrobats and quack doctors of the fair. A nearer parallel
is between Concanen and Jacques Callot. The engravings
by Callot and by his pupil Stefano della Bella that show a
single comedian standing in enormous proportion before us
against a background of buildings and little figures, often
with the remainder of the troupe dancing or walking on
stilts far away in the distance down the piazza, near a fountain
or a colonnade, these compare, except in point of Italian
exaggeration, with *The Bond Street Beau*. We can tell that
resemblance, even in his eyes. To the crown of his top hat
he is the height, we noticed, of the Bond Street buildings.
His figure fills the entire street from cellar to attic. He is
in the direct tradition, without knowing it, from Callot.
Tradition, or else expediency, for it is a convention that
comes from close observation of actors in the theatre. For
they are seen in curious perspective on the open stage,
against the scene, and transferred out of the theatre into
ordinary life they are not as other persons. The peculiarities
of their profession cling to them and do not leave them. Just
as, were we to see *The Bond Street Beau* upon the boards, we
would enter into the spirit and believe, for the moment, that
he was really walking up and down the Bond Street pavement. So were we to meet him, say between Atkinson's
scent shop and Piccadilly, our thoughts would immediately
transfer him to the theatre and to the music of his song.
Thus, in either half of his life he is unreal and dependant
upon conditions or circumstances of exaggeration.

This was an environment that suited the temperament

of Concanen, perhaps prone to exaggeration, racially, and no lover of the sober truth. But his imagination worked in fantasy. There is no melodrama in Concanen, and only invention based upon possibility, springing in many instances from a mere literal translation of the words or situations in a song. As an artist, we will next ask who were the aristocrats of his profession ? He drew song covers for the music publishers, but it is probable he envied the artists who made drawings for the illustrated weekly papers. Their sketches were transferred to wood by other hands, for seldom, if ever, did they print their own woodcuts. By now, a very high standard of reproduction had been attained, as witness the beautiful woodcuts of the 'sixties. Only a few years earlier, little if anything of the artist's personality survived after his sketches had been handed to the engraver, the proof of which is the practical impossibility of identifying the drawings by Constantin Guys furnished by that most personal of draughtsmen to the early numbers of the *Illustrated London News*. His sketches of the Crimean War differ hardly at all from those of any other war correspondent, however highly characterized they may have been in their originals. But the status of Concanen as popular artist in the fullest meaning of the term, and the peculiar or very special limits of his opportunity, put him in company with another popular and highly specialized artist, at the far side of the world. The main difference between them is not one of degree, but only in the fact that collectors will pay hundreds of pounds for a single woodcut by the Oriental master while his London equivalent and parallel can be picked up for a few shillings.

This ghost or echo of Concanen, to whom he so nearly corresponds in everything but a close similarity, is the Japanese artist Sharaku. He is well known for his grimacing heads of actors, often with a silver or a mica background.

The circumstances of Sharaku are peculiar in the extreme. A little over one hundred woodcuts are known by him, one hundred and eight to be exact, and it would appear that he worked during the last ten months, only, of 1794. He was a No dancer, by profession, in the service of a daimyo, but after this fantastic spate of drawing he returned to his ordinary means of livelihood and kept a fish stall. The setting is a close parallel to the whelks and winkles and the oyster stalls of the music-hall public of Victorian London, nor is *The Dark Girl Dress'd in Blue* in her immense crinoline any less improbable than figures in the streets or theatres of the cities of Japan. But the quality of Sharaku, whose woodcuts are so highly prized, lies in his portrayal of melodrama and in his powers of "psychological violence". This is expressed in the hands of his actors with their clenched or contorted fingers, in their furious grimaces, and in the loud explosions of the patterns on their coloured dresses. In his own time, and it was certainly the shortest period ever allotted to any artist, Sharaku was an unknown draughtsman who took sketches of the actors in cheap theatres. He did not carve the wood blocks. They were carried out by the professional engravers, who did the printing. In method of representation they are entirely different, but closely alike in degree and circumstance, to the best of Concanen's music covers, which is to say that his masterpieces, *The Age of Paper* and *What Our Swells Are Coming To !*, as lithographs, are as much works of art as Sharaku's woodcuts. And the fine prints of Concanen cover almost as short a period as the ten months of Sharaku, being produced with hardly an exception between 1861 and 1863.

But we proceed, immediately, with *The Hansom Galop*, one of the most extreme of Concanen's music covers, a work most contingent to our preceding paragraph, for in manner and in unfamiliar queerness it has a near resemblance to the Japanese. Not at all, though, to the actors of Sharaku's prints, but rather to the ' action pictures ', flights and battle paintings of an earlier age, and in particular to the astonishing twelfth-century scroll painting of the battle and burning of the palace, by Minamoto, which forms one of the sensations of Fenollosa's wonderful *Epochs of Chinese and Japanese Art*. This depicts fire, flight, and panic, and the confusion and running of many hundreds of white-clad warriors, all in their black-lacquered hats, amid rearing horses and runaway two-wheeled carriages, a masterpiece of a curious kind, for so violent is the action that it approaches the stylized animation of a ' crazy cartoon ', with so many of its figures in simultaneous action, running, fighting, panicking among the flames. *The Hansom Galop* has not fallen as far as that into caricature, but its top hats, its whirling wheels and plunging horses, are in analogy only to the Tosa school. Red wheels and a yellow hansom cab are in the foreground, drawn by a little white mare at full gallop, which is the story. For we are to presume that it is a private hansom. I am old enough to remember very well indeed the sensation of driving in a hansom, of the high climb into that upright gondola, a feeling that was almost like mounting a horse, the leathern cabin, and then the closing of the apron flaps. I can remember for contrast the *fiacres* of the Paris streets, with no character but the glazed bowler hats, black for winter, white in summer, of the cabmen. The hansom was peculiar to London, and at the corner of South Audley Street I recall the swift passing of a private hansom, a young man sitting inside it, and my mother telling me to whom it belonged, not so long ago, even, that this famous character is not still alive and flourishing. By some unwritten law, the private hansoms were painted black as their prototype the public hansom, they were as funereal as the Venetian gondola, but in the instance before us this sumptuary law

48

or regulation has been abated and it has scarlet wheels and a bright yellow cabin.

But we will describe it in detail. Yellow shafts and yellow apron flaps ; little windows at each side, for privacy, with scarlet curtains of the same colour as the wheels, and over the window the painted insignia of a red fox in clue to its sporting owner or inhabitant. Above the roof of the cab, in mid-air, appears the private cabman, bluff but serene, with flying whiskers and flying coat tails. He is wearing, in fact, a padded overcoat with heavy brass buttons, a blue muffler with white polka dots, a red rose in his buttonhole, and a very special or particular top hat, a hat only worn, indeed, by the driver of a private hansom, for it has a tall, bulbous crown and a boat-shaped or curving brim, a hat over life size, and altogether too large for its owner till we see the way it rides from long use upon his puffs of hair. We should know, could we see nothing else of him than his coat tails and his coat sleeves, that this is a cabman, but there is, as well, his red velvet waistcoat. There must be tailors in some quarter of London who make the cabmen's over-coats. As he sits up there above the bright yellow cabin, with dangling lamp swaying from its bracket and the loose reins to either side of it, all else that we have time to notice is the long whip in his hand, for he has just cracked his whip and the long lash of it, like some great calligraphic flourish, flies off into the light-blue lettering of *The Hansom Galop*, darts in and out through the openings of the A's and O's, and like the vapour trail of an aeroplane against a cloudless sky leads into the distance, but a few feet away, where the passage of this bright red and yellow curricle, or call it the pouncing music of *The Hansom Galop*, has reared up a nag in terror, broken the wheels off another hansom, and hurled both driver and passenger head first, but we see one rising and the other falling, to the ground. At their back two more hansoms, one behind the other, their whip-lashes writing other calligraphic figures upon the empty air. All we see are the cabmen's coats, the common cabmen's coats in many tiers, and the high box seat or chair of one of them, a throne on which to sit with many rugs wrapped round the feet in winter, a driver's seat the world over, for it may remind us of the old two-wheeled carts, now vanished, that carried wine from the vineyards of the Castelli Romani into the streets of Rome, carts with a hooded seat at one side for the driver, and always a barking dog upon the wine barrels, and many pots and pans hanging down between the axles, slow moving, and like an untidy, overcrowded house or tent on wheels. To the other side, the same story. A horse fallen on its front knees, the driver falling head-foremost, and his passenger thrown forward with hands outstretched to catch his top hat. Behind him a mufflered cabman making off as best he can, cracking his whip, his frightened horse with distraught mane trying to look round, and scenting trouble. In the foreground, two dogs running away from the scarlet wheels as fast as they can go.

And the owner or inhabitant of the yellow hansom with the red wheels ? He is sitting, bolt upright, with hands folded and resting on the yellow apron, quite indifferent to the confusion and stampede that he is causing. We only see his bust, as it were, and not lower than his elbows, but he is dressed in a light-blue overcoat, or a jacket made like an overcoat, with puffy sleeves, and fastening with one button only ; a black velvet collar to his coat ; a red cravat or necktie ; an expanse of white waistcoat ; and then his folded hands in gloves. He is staring straight in front of him, smoking a cigar or cheroot, and with his eyeglass in his eye. He wears a grey top hat, almost brimless, with a black band, a top hat of the sort without a curve, and with straight sides. A fair-haired dude, with hair and whiskers

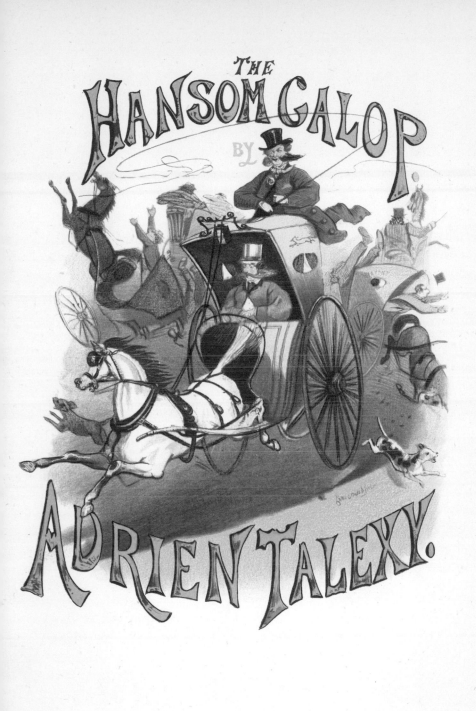

made stiff with pomade or bear's grease, a fair moustache, and hair that, besides being curled heavily and elaborately above his ears, is combed straight out at the sides in the fashion there has never been before or since, flowing whiskers, they are, that reach to either side beyond his shoulders, adding to the impression that he gives of oblivious hurry. He must be wearing light-coloured trousers, 'peg-top' trousers cut close and tapering to his ankles, but baggy at the knees, and exhibiting in their curious cut the taste and flavour of the time, so that it would be a delight to watch him step down, to hear him speak a few words in his fashionable drawl, and see him walk along the pavement. But he never moves or stirs. The tail of his white mare streams out against the black splashboard of the hansom, a splashboard of an individual shape quite different from those that I remember, for it resembles the ghost of the back of a chair, and behind it, protected again by the yellow apron, he sits upright, passing by quickly on his way — to where ? It is none of our business. But to talk inanities at a champagne luncheon in an oyster bar. No ! It is the wrong time of day. This is the late afternoon. More likely, then, to the stage door of the theatre. Or to his club, where he will stand in his top hat in front of the empty fireplace talking to other young men of his own pattern, drinking a brandy and soda and glancing at the papers.

Like a fly in amber this whiskered dude is embalmed for ever in his yellow hansom, but it is an immortality of a peculiar kind, for nothing could be more temporary or impermanent than an old music cover. But he is immortal in the sense that nothing else can give us to such an extent as this the flesh and blood of the past, and the fleeting moment. The most painstaking of the Pre-Raphaelites must fail beside Concanen. Saved from Victorian sentimentality by the jargon of the music hall and by the actors, male and female, whom he frequented, this forgotten artist shows us a side of life that is ignored completely in the woodcuts to *Good Words* or *Once a Week* and that we could never find in the novels of Anthony Trollope or George Eliot. It is the slang world of *Paul Pry* and other scurrilous publications and of complications that were seldom reported in the newspapers. Not the world of grand opera, of ballet, or of pantomime, but, in fact, the illegitimate, not the legitimate stage and a world that extended from mere vocalists and singers of sentimental ballads to comedians and eccentrics of near genius. Not, indeed, that their merits were more than an occasional spur to Concanen, for we may guess that he was forced by circumstances to take his opportunity where he found it. *The Hansom Galop* is but one of a hundred similar pieces by Adrien Talexy. The catalogues of the old music publishers are full of them, but we are to opine that this Irishman from Co. Galway felt grand that morning. After a dose of the poison that was, eventually, to clog his genius and kill him ? We cannot tell ; but it is not improbable. For *The Hansom Galop* is a free flight of fancy. It depicts no particular person, unless it be Concanen himself. There is only the suggestion of the title. A name, like so many more, but it has inspired him to the transcendental.

A trite, insipid galop, of no importance in itself. We may doubt whether Concanen had ever heard the tune. It is more probable that some other, better galop or polka was in his head from the night before, for his drawing is like the mental image of a tune. This image has seized the characteristic, which is the pouncing rhythm, a trotting or galloping horse-galop, this is it, and not quite a polka. How much could be written upon the waltzes and polkas of the time ! How quickly we may tell male and female in the four or six or eight successive tunes or phases of a waltz by Strauss ! The men and women of Waldteufel's valses are not less easily to be distinguished. But where we are concerned with London, and with the particular English or even cockney style in dancing, it is to be realized that the popular taste was for the polka. Of this it could be said without exaggeration that there were the American, French, and German schools, with the London or English, as ever, holding the balance between the others, but with an individuality of their own. I would point to an American influence in the drawing for *The Hansom Galop*, remembering that so typical a London portrait as Lord Dundreary was created and played a thousand times in America before it was brought to England, and that, regarding Concanen the Irishman, the United States during the two decades of the 'fifties and 'sixties, after the famine, had become the home of some millions of emigrants from Ireland. The American accent in speech and music had set foot in our music halls. I am thinking less of the Nigger Minstrels than of the vaudeville turns, acrobats, dancers, and the like, from the United States who must, already, have had a musical language of their own. A music that follows the intonations of the spoken word and that abounds, by now, in cliché and in set convention. But, also, in strokes of inspiration so that someone with a lifetime of experience of these tunes would have his memory stored with the whole repertory of their turns of phrase. When shorn of its sentiment, purged of its banalities, this music is as rich and varied as the Spanish tunes, pasadobles and dances of the zarzuela, that, all unknowing, were among the minor wonders of the nineteenth century. From such fantasies was born this beau in his blue ' reefer ' coat and white top hat driving, so inanely and furiously, in his yellow hansom with the scarlet wheels. Concanen's epitome of the whiskered dude of the eighteensixties ; but more curious is yet to come.

The Age of Paper may be the masterpiece of Concanen. It

is assuredly among the most beautiful of coloured lithographs, signed Concanen and Lee, like *Kleptomania*, a partnership which may account for the superlative excellence of the colouring. Copies of this rare music cover may vary a good deal in impression, but that in the British Museum never fails to strike anew with its brilliance. Here is the portrait of a fop or dude done with no satirical intention. For there is more than that behind the immaculate swagger of *The Bond Street Beau*. It will not be long before this latter is a guest for the night at Vine Street, and appears next morning before the Magistrate. A walking model of tailoring, nevertheless, from Conduit Street or Savile Row, and we would turn back and look again at his top hat, a face, for that moment, like a tame lion in a top hat, his waisted short coat, flecked strawberry-roan trousers, and tasselled walking-stick. A drawing inspired by music, for who can doubt that Concanen's head rang with music while he made the sketch ! Look at the waist of *The Bond Street Beau*, the walk, the space between his right arm and leg, the languid gloved left hand ! But *The Age of Paper* is more serious in intention. Not an instance of musical intoxication, of the catalepsis, the arrested moment. Instead, it is drawn with affection, with loving care. It is as though Concanen had wished to leave this portrait of one of the extreme props of fashion. Upon a mere music cover, to be turned over in haste, and torn, each time the music is opened upon the piano ? But the artist had no alternative. He could not have expected his works to live for more than a few months, or a year or two, and then to join the old newspapers and be thrown out with the rags and rubbish. The very impermanence of the old music cover makes the more magical this survival of the elegancies of that long-lost age.

We see before us a young man of about twenty-four years of age, standing in inimitable attitude twirling the end of his moustache between the thumb and finger of one hand. His top hat, worn at just the right angle, is of the purest water, a hat which connoisseurs will distinguish at once from the top hat of *The Bond Street Beau*, for the brim is flatter and it does not taper in the crown. How fine it rides upon his curled forelock ! This young man has blue eyes and his face is very pink and white. The shade of his hat brim only makes this the more evident. His fair side-whiskers are combed out so that they flow over and beyond his shoulders. And from his head downwards we begin to get the significance of *The Age of Paper*. For the shop window behind him advertises Paper Hats, Paper Collars, Paper Coats ; and we see Paper Men, Paper Wigs, Paper Knives and Stockings, Paper Buckets and Umbrellas, more top hats of paper, and a row of women's paper bonnets. The street post, as inevitable of the London streets as those in *Kleptomania* and in *The Bond Street Beau*, has bills pasted upon it of Il Papa di Roma just out, and of Mr. Howard Paul, *The Age of Paper*, in a Paper Suit To Night, together with Paper Hanging, cheapest in London. We see a newsboy to one side of him, calling out the *Daily Telegraph* ; and to the other side a small boy in a flat cap flying a paper kite. The tail of the kite with its twists of paper resembles a musical score as it trails in front of a further window, with Papeterie and Papier Maché billed upon it ; and the colours are brilliant. There is a red face painted on the paper kite ; the shop lettering is in red, so are the ladies' bonnets in the window, and the newsboy has a red waistcoat. In the far corner, two Jews in the ubiquitous top hat must be discussing paper money.

Now we can return to the beau himself, who leans with his right hand on a long, bright scarlet walking stick. Could it be a stick of papier maché, or of some bright red composition ? For he is dressed from head to foot in paper.

His coat and trousers, in themselves, are masterpieces. The coat is yellowish-brown with red buttons, but of most fashionable and elegant material, cut, we may flatter ourselves, as only the tailors of London know the secret, edged with a black braid, and with a black velvet collar. There are red and blue buttons, alternately, upon his waistcoat, and the flaps of his waistcoat have rolled ends, which, alone, betray the secret, for they are dog's ears, exactly like the rolled edges or corners of a sheet of paper, but we find it difficult to look away from his coat, so perfect in fit and elegant in shape, fastened by one button only, and falling away so easily below his hip and half-way to his knee, a coat which is exactly right in length and colour, perfectly proportioned to his head and whiskers, to his top hat and long red walking stick. In his coat pocket there is a frilled handkerchief, beautifully folded, till we see that it is only a paper napkin. However, the most touching traces of time in this portrait of a beau we find to be in the peculiar length of his coat, in his shoulders, and in the wonderful foreshortened drawing of his raised left arm and sleeve. A coat that in cut and material could pertain to no other time at all, so that it is true to call it a lost secret while we admire its length and waist and admit that these are contrived by instinct to suit his top hat and whiskers, his trousers and his boots. This coat and the whole image of this dandy are a sartorial invention, by which we mean that his clothes are so carefully drawn that they must have existed in the original and Concanen cannot have created them. They are the authentic clothes of a beau or dandy of the time and without historic parallel, any more than the hansom cab is copied from the vehicle of any other time or place. We may say, even, that we have seen no other shoulders like his shoulders. And as we look at his velvet coat collar in order to examine his necktie, we see that he has a blue tie, but that the clasp or fastening of his stiff

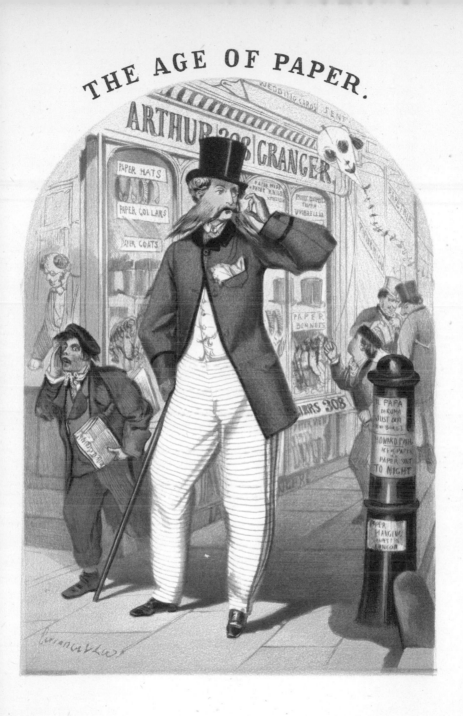

collar is nothing else than a red postage stamp. We know the youthful head of Queen Victoria facing to the right, but this little joke on the part of the artist, this little allusion to *The Age of Paper*, has jumped forward three-quarters of a century to the symbols or images of a Salvador Dali or an Yves Tanguy. *The Age of Paper* becomes a work that would be accepted by the Surrealists and that could be exalted into a criticism of the Reign of Mammon.

The raised left arm of the beau, lifted in order that he should curl the end of his moustaches between his thumb and finger, shows the line of braid upon his cuff, but it is important by reason of the superb drawing of his elbow and upper sleeve, a feat accomplished by treating it as a kind of geometrical figure, the base or three sides of a hexagon narrowing into the plain tube of his cuff, but with the seam or line showing, and in the other direction widening by an arc and another span or stay into his armpit. Above his shoulder, touching it and brushing it, there are his whiskers, the corn-coloured whiskers and moustaches of this pink-and-white-faced dandy. It is curious, indeed, to look at the elegance of the strand of moustache between his thumb and finger and at his pomaded curls, remembering that so much moustache and whisker only became fashionable after two winters spent in redoubts and trenches in the Crimean War, and that as quickly as this, within a decade, those Polar explorers, for such is their appearance in the early photographs, have refined down to this. For he stands there, forgetting the beaux of other centuries, or never having heard of them, while only a foot or two away from him, in commentary, there flies the red-and-white face painted on the kite, with a boy running in front of, but controlling it, who will grow up into a man.

How superb and mannered are his trousers ! They are white, with blue ruled lines, and red transverse lines running down the seam only of his left leg. These trousers are incomparable in drawing. In the whole of fashion drawing we can think of nothing finer ; not even in the rare male figures in Gavarni's fashion plates. But they are the trousers, particularly, of a London beau or dandy. The Paris tailors could never cut or fit like this. And it only now dawns on us that they are paper trousers, that they are cut out of the ruled paper in an office account book. We do not know which leg to admire most. For the beau is standing for a moment at the street corner. His weight is on his left leg and he leans on his red walking stick. The modelling of the blue ruled lines, giving even more of elegance to the white summer material, carries down from his hip and stomach, in itself a difficult technical passage, without sagging or bulging to his knee, and then continues to his neat black shoes of inimitable London make, and we have to look up again at this tower of elegance, to watch him twirl his moustache, and to catch the gleam of summer weather on his black top hat. His other leg is more foreshortened, probably even more difficult of execution. It drops down straight and rigid from below the fork, narrows at the knee, with a subtlety of drawing that one would have thought only a Frenchman, an artist of the delicate blood of Watteau, would have understood, for there is no narrowing of the blue ruled lines but the foot of the trouser tapers with no awkwardness, and where it meets the shoe, does so in a manner that is the signature of the moment, for we could even date the drawing within a year or two from his trouser end and from the angle at which it rides upon his shoe. This pair of trousers, in themselves, suggest a civilization and an elegance of their own. How rakish, but unexaggerated, the angle of his top hat and what invention in his coat length ! For the coat, as worn now, and probably standardized for ever, does not permit of any effect at all, and remark that this dandy's coat is not an overcoat. Neither is it a frock coat ; nor a tail coat. We admire, as we have said, the way in which it fastens with one button, and is intended, there below, to hang permanently unbuttoned, with a line like a subtle ' cut-away ', but designed, therefore, either for an immaculate pair of trousers of the same material, in which event we should have the beau appearing as a brown-yellow ' self ', red or yellow in the language of the pigeon fancy, for he would be whole-coloured as a red or yellow Jacobin or Archangel ; or for summer trousers like this pair of white cloth, with ruled blue lines and red lines down the seams.

A young man, we know it at once, different in ante-cedents from *The Bond Street Beau*. For that was an actor ; or if not the portrait of the comedian himself, at any rate of someone pretending to be important, but who lived, really, in a shabby lodging. What wonderful pictures Concanen has left to us of the ' swells ' upon the London streets ! We are beginning to understand that the ubiquitous black coat and top hat permitted of a hundred subtle changes in the colour and shape of hat, the length and colour of coat. Mr Howard Paul, " attired in a suit of paper ", who sang the song, does not resemble the drawings upon other of his song covers. We may think it more probable that the ' swell ' of *The Age of Paper* was a peer's son or baronet, frequenter of the music halls, and acquaintance or companion of Concanen. They will have had drinks together in the glare of the great gas chandeliers. Or because there is no mockery of the ' swell ', and he is presented so seriously, it may be that the dandy of *The Age of Paper* is what the artist would have liked, himself, to be, but given the form of some acquaint-ance, improved, as it were, or in fact, idealized. How else are we to explain why there is no note of satire in *The Age of Paper* ? For nothing is exaggerated, not even when we know

E

the curious fantasy of the drawing and are able to convince ourselves that his entire suit is made of paper. Indeed he does not appear in that light at all. He remains a ' swell ' of 1863 dressed in the height of fashion. A member, is it not probable, of the newly founded Marlborough Club, habitué of the Landseer print and horsehair sofa ? With young appetite (we have guessed that he is not more than twenty-four years old), a lover of oysters, of marrow bones and mutton chops, and who for his breakfast will consume a grilled sole and a dish of crumpets and quince jam. A smoker of cigars and cheroots, for cigarettes are not yet known, and who spends much time at the cigar merchant's and at the tailor's. At the happiest time of his life, for fashion changes. And in another year or two all fantasy had fled. It may be that we see him at almost the last summer in which such colours were allowed for coat and trousers.

But these ' swells ' of London, one and all, have this purity or integrity of breeding that they are completely unaffected by aesthetics. The image, in its variety, is incontaminate and uncorrupted. There is no apeing of any historical style. This is the image reared by the subconscious to walk beside the crinoline. But the crinoline is of French and Spanish origin ; French, because the Empress Eugénie affected the modes and manners of Marie-Antoinette, and Spanish, because the Empress was by birth a Spaniard, in an age, curiously, when only Manet and a few others had found the paintings of Velasquez. The Emperor Napoleon, walking beside the Empress, wore a frock coat and ' stovepipe ' hat of English make ; coat and trousers from Savile Row, shoes from a London shoemaker, and his tall top hat, we doubt not, from Lock the hatter in St James's Street. Even so the Emperor did not look a Londoner. But he wore the London livery.

But we would walk behind the beau or ' swell ' and see

him from the back, in a view that, had this been a drawing of fashion and no more, would have been realized close beside him, for he would have been drawn both back and front. As we turn him round, in imagination, we see the double strings of the monocle in his left eye, another proof of the 'good taste' of the drawing, for it is the first time we have noticed that he wears an eyeglass. The view of him from the back is interesting because this is a statue meant to be seen from all angles and to move among the crowd. Now we can examine him, from his long back hair brushed upwards as though drawn by a vortex or inrush of air into his hat, to his narrow shoulders, made narrower by the black velvet coat collar, and may admire the back of his coat, of exact length and fit, rehearsed many times and altered before the tailor's mirror. It could have been designed, purposely, to move slowly as male escort to the crinoline. More far-fetched than the crinoline, for he is without antecedent. None have ever seen his like. The man, more than the woman, was the invention of the age.

And now, if we are to be allowed some meeting, some clash of personalities, let it be that this paragon takes but a languid step or two and comes face to face with *The Bond Street Beau*. We are waiting for him as though trying to remember some old, old tune. And here he comes, looming large as the houses on the other side of the street, one of the ghosts of music, for it is sufficient to sing a bar or two to ourselves, and he appears. Automaton-like, he will even answer to several tunes, so long, only, as they are in his character. For, in fact, we do not know the music of *The Bond Street Beau*. It is only a loose cover torn away from its words and music. But the drawing chooses its own music. It dictates it as surely as the words direct a song, while the 'swell' of *The Age of Paper* needs, as it were, no music, or nothing more than a phrase or comment. He is for ever striking his attitude, while the other walks his beat along the pavement. One thing is certain, that they will never meet ; that they will show no recognition of each other ; that they will no more go up and speak to each other than officers in the same regiment, or members of the same club. The barriers dividing them are rules of caste, to the degree that they might drink together under the same roof, without speaking, but could never sit down, willingly, to the same meal. And both of them, even as a very few old gentlemen to this day, would sit and eat without removing their top hats. Such could be the personal terms of two men-about-town who pass each other ten or twenty times a day, and who are not even curious to enquire each other's secrets ; who could spend a lifetime without asking for a name, or looking for an address. Not that they are not interested. But it is a point of honour.

If, as we could wish, all or any of our pages, indoors or out, down Bond Street or before the painted scene, are impregnated with the light airs of the theatre and the music hall, then it is no difficult transition from the fantastic elegant of *The Age of Paper* to the pure fantasy of *What Our Swells Are Coming To !* This was sung by Mr Howard Paul in the above " Get-Up ". It is, therefore, a portrait taken direct, signed Alfred Concanen, and the lithography was his own work entirely, unaided by the professionals. There is no background, but only a blue scumbling, the light blue of the lithographer's pencil, reaching to the elbows of the extraordinary figure who stands before us and projecting him, therefore, as though standing on a patch of ground against a cerulean sky. Nothing of the theatre, or of the footlights, but it is conveyed to us that he comes before us as a messenger, that he has alighted out of the air, that he is, as it were, the Mercury of fashion, who runs before to tell its changes. We look for the wand in his hand, and for his winged hat or sandals. From the way he stands, from the attitude of his whole body, and his outstretched hands, he has begun his song. We see it, too, in his parted lips and staring eyes.

We will look at him, as we would Mercury, from his winged sandals, upwards. He is wearing black shoes with square toes, a style that persisted for a few years, and red heels. He has black-and-white striped socks and his black shoes have excessive bows. Not less peculiar, therefore, than Mercury's winged sandals, for it is many thousands of years since, if ever, those fluttered at his heels. For trousers this 'swell of swells' is wearing corded tights of yellow nankeen, but it has nothing to do with corduroy. They are not ribbed ; they are only corded at the sides with a black cord, where the braid runs on black evening trousers. His pantaloons are skin-tight, and at the hip they have a curious projecting ear or flap for convenience in fastening the loops of seals or bangles. The effect of his nankeen pantaloons is that he is wearing trousers made of chamois leather, and two big seals swing from a broad black ribbon on his left-hand side.

The coat worn by this extraordinary figure is a green velvet jacket fastened by two great buttons. But it has the widest and most extravagant of lapels, faced with light green silk, and cut so that the extreme points are far wider than his shoulders and he appears to be emerging out of some huge green leaf. His shoulders are invisible. They are working under that cut leaf of a tulip tree. But the lapels allow for a wide shirt opening and for the emergence of an enormous collar. The stiff shirt front, buckling in the middle, is patterned with two rows of round black dots, while the collar above that, which covers him from neck to chin, has four of the same dots, with a fifth dot in the middle, in illustration of the couplet :

> And collars once so free from blots,
> Have burst out in a rash of spots.

We are to imagine, therefore, that such spotted collars had become the fashion, though the rage lasted for so short a time that there is no other trace left of it, while the preceding couplet :

> Shirt fronts one in amazement views,
> All foxes heads or horses shoes

is given veracity by another couplet that reads :

> White neckties fasten'd thro' a ring,
> Have dwindled down to bits of string,

for the ' swell of swells ' wears no tie at all, though his front stud is to be seen. Anything so ephemeral as the fancy shirts " All foxes heads or horses shoes " will have perished or been thrown away after a winter or a summer so that the only witness to their existence would be in cartoons or comic papers. The green velvet sleeves of his jacket end in stiff shirt cuffs with the black dots in pattern of fives as on his collar; the ' swell of swells ' wears pale-green gloves, holds in his right hand a toy gallows with a small doll in a crinoline dangling from it, and in his left hand, or rather, perched on his green-gloved index finger, a doll, two or three inches high, consisting of a pink-crinolined young lady, her skirt blown out behind her, the ribbons of her bonnet blowing in the breeze, and holding in her hand a pale-pink parasol. The head of this statue of a dude or ' swell ' is of a furious inanity. He has a pink and white complexion denoting youth, for the whiskered dudes of the 'sixties are perennially young, as witness the line :

> At thirty they're considered old ;

he wears a monocle with an enormous double string, and is on this occasion not bearded but has a positively immense pair of moustaches flowing out over his collar and brushed up at the ends.

> Their hats, once tow'ring to the skies
> Are now as flat as mutton-pies !

refers to the tall ' stove-pipe ' hats that were at one time the fashion in the 'sixties and that are to be seen, invariably, in photographs of Napoleon III, either worn on his head to accentuate his height, or on occasion placed, curiously, on his knee or on the table at his side. The hat of the ' swell of swells ', obeying the couplet, is a very low-crowned grey top hat with a black band and with the most curving of brims, the brim, moreover, as with certain parti-coloured flowers, pinks or roses, being white above, and the ground colour, black in this instance, on the underneath. But we must look at the border, too, of the drawing, for the fantasy is not yet complete. It has a nondescript rough frame or edging in the rococo of the mirror frame, and of no moment, but to the sides, and touching this border, there are two groups of objects. To the right it is a long thin cheroot, with a long ash burning, tied with ribbons to a walking stick, without a handle, but from which hangs another doll in a white bodice and rose-pink crinoline. To the left it is more interesting. There is a tall barber's block, we can see the round base of it, and a dummy human head mounted with a wig, brushed, no doubt, after the fashion of the ' swell of swells '; but this barber's block has had a stiff shirt front and collar tried on it, a collar even more outrageous than that of the ' swell ' himself, for it covers where the dummy's ears should be, the pattern, both on shirt front and collar, consisting of cockroaches or blackbeetles scuttling in all directions. Below this, marked " 7/6 Tres chic ", and lying partly on the ground, there is a shirt front of another pattern, for you can see the loop to fasten it, but, strictly speaking, it has wings and not a collar ; it is intended, therefore, for some bow or cravat to go above it. This shirt front, which is unstarched, is of powder-blue material and it has a design of ballet dancers' legs and shoes, their pointed feet kicking uniformly in pattern, and in the midst, where should be the pink ballet skirt or *tutu*, the apology for this flimsy garment, and on that a great toad crawling, the edges of the shirt with more dancers' feet kicking into it, and the wings for the collar having one arched foot and instep to either side completing the design.

This astonishing short-coated 'swell' is of a type that existed certainly. He appears in *La Vie Parisienne* of Offenbach, in the two young men Gardefeu and Bobinet who are pacing up and down in the opening scene at the Gare St Lazare. Gardefeu, we have to quote from our own previous description, " has the tall ' stove-pipe ' hat or ' cylindre ', pomaded hair, a monocle, a walking stick with a tassel, and wears the latest elegance of a short brown coat, trousers of the same, and a fancy waistcoat ". A short coat, we remark, but not yet the pea-jacket. Bobinet, however, " le petit Bob ", " wears a short coat that is like an Eton jacket ". This may be seen in photographs and drawings of the first performance of *La Vie Parisienne* in 1867. And the fancy shirts of *What Our Swells Are Coming To !* are no more improbable and no less likely to be true. We have to accept, therefore, that such figures or their near equivalent were to be seen. We know, even, that the extremes in actual life are more exaggerated than their portrayal in the theatre, and that D'Orsay or Brummel should never be put upon the stage.

This may be, it almost certainly is, the most extreme of music-hall song covers by Concanen. Not as beautiful in quality as *The Age of Paper*, but more fantastic. But this raises the question of what proportion of his output we have been able to see : there are many difficulties in the way of collectors, not least that in the library of the British Museum the songs are catalogued under their composers' names, and that in those many hundreds or even thousands of items there is no clue whatever as to whether the cover will be by Concanen, or not, and as little as to what its merits or qualities may be. Months or years could be spent making an aesthetic arrangement of his covers, grouping and comparing them, and I have not had time to devote more than a few weeks to this labour. Certain of his transcendental drawings could appear, unexpected and un-heralded, at any moment in a long life. I am unwilling to believe, though, that any could be better than *Klepto-mania* or *The Age of Paper*.

One of the latest covers by Concanen must be an amusing travesty of the aesthetic movement, with a young man closely resembling J. M. Whistler standing in a velveteen jacket with clasped hands in adoration before a sunflower, and with vases of the beloved Nankin or blue-and-white china in the background. The chorus of this song has the refrain, " We are all too utterly utter ". It is an echo of the Grosvenor Gallery of the late 'seventies and early 'eighties ; and, in conclusion, what few personal details we have of the artist may be summed up by saying that we know one person, an assistant in a famous London gallery, who remem-bers Concanen from having been apprenticed in his youth to a firm of lithographers. Concanen was old and ill, then, and not much is recounted of him beyond the informa-tion that he had been a leading figure in the London Irish Volunteers. Charles Coborn, " the man who broke the bank at Monte Carlo ", the veteran music-hall singer who died in 1945, and who was drawn by Concanen, upon enquiry knew his name well but had never met him. Concanen seems to be mentioned, but with his name mis-spelt, in a cryptic and somewhat unsavoury episode referred to by Lafourcade in his book on Swinburne, or so much can be surmised reading between the lines ; and I have been shown a characteristic and amusing letter from Gordon Craig describing a meeting or encounter with him. To conclude, I should add that I have seen more than one book with illustrations by Concanen, but that none of them are of any merit. I have seen, also, a great number of his bad or mediocre song covers. And this is all I know about him.

We are left, though, with the phenomenon of how good a draughtsman Concanen could be, upon occasion. And, after a long day, we are reflecting upon this as the lamplighter runs past and the lamps are lit. Or it could be that we come out of the music hall into the crowded streets. And for this, Concanen being no more our guide, we have sought another witness. We find him in the person of a draughtsman who is anonymous, and likely to remain so. All that we know is that he was a French tutor in an English family, and a large album of his drawings came into our possession a few years ago. It may be remembered that Constantin Guys occupied the same position in the family of the proprietors of the *Illustrated London News,* and that owing to this he was given the post of war correspondent or war artist to that paper in the Crimean War. Without in any way comparing them to each other, for Guys was among the great draughtsmen of all time and the other a mere amateur, it is sufficient to remark that their circumstances were the same. But Guys belonged, of course, to an earlier generation. The time that we are speaking of, when he was tutor, was in the early 'forties, while the majority of drawings in our album are dated 1868.

It is a large folio, marked *Souvenirs d'Angleterre : Personnages,* and opens with a lithograph of *Smith's Advertizing Station* which is pasted on to the front page. This is, in fact, a wooden hoarding covered from top to bottom with advertisements, after the fashion of the drop scene lowered during the interval in suburban and provincial music halls. They are in white, and green, and red, and blue, and yellow, and are cross readings, intended to be read downwards, so as to get a series of incongruities. We read : Vote for B. Disraeli, Christy's Minstrels, Sims Reeves, Rev. C. H. Spurgeon, The Pope and the King of Naples, Madam Celeste, and The Devil on Two Sticks, and there is no other object in the lithograph except, at the right-hand side, the green pillar of a London lamp-post. The first drawing, on the next page, is an interior in pencil, marked Dublin, 1860, and without interest save for a row of chairs, for what used to be called a Sutherland table, and a gas chandelier. We pass on : there is an interior of a bedroom, with the bed in full colour : and on the next page a wash-stand and a chest of drawers, but marked *Southampton*, and drawn, perhaps, in a hotel bedroom on a rainy day. Next, there come drawings of soldiers ; some Highlanders (these would amuse a Frenchman) ; Dover, 1857 ; infantry in red coats, still wearing the shako of the Peninsular War ; some sailors, tough and bearded, straw-hatted, and smoking long clay pipes ; Turkish sailors (1858), not long after the Crimean War, in red tarbushes with blue tassels ; and the band of the Royal Marines, all in white, with red pipings and red epaulettes. Next, the Gypsies, in three drawings ; followed by three ladies of fashion on one page, ladies in flounced crinolines, at Portsmouth, and the wives or daughters, probably, of naval officers.

The next drawing is of four women in crinolines with long braided surcoats, giving them a severe appearance. They wear flat tambour hats with red plumes, and their chignons are hanging in gold-spotted snoods. The pages following are uninteresting, till we come to a drawing,

Dublin, of two women in crinolines of Irish green with long black cloaks and mantles, and on the next sheet a beggar woman, smoking a pipe and staring at a lady in the height of fashion. Four terrifying beggars come next, or they are three ' sandwich women ' and a man, all barefoot, dressed in rags. The woman on the left, with tousled fair hair and spectacles, knits a stocking, but her needles are more like straws. Her companion, too, holds knitting needles, but they suggest the straws that lunatics used to weave or play with when they were manacled and left to lie in darkness upon beds of straw. The newspaper placard boy is dressed from head to foot in rags with large spaces showing at his knees and arms. Whenever I look at the drawing of him I am reminded of the only barefoot children I have ever seen in England, playing in front of the black stone town hall of Sheffield when I was a child. I have since felt certain that they were part of the local Irish population, there being a low Irish quarter as in Liverpool. What I remember are their frayed trouser ends and the thought of the appalling brick courts and kennels where they must live.

But the anonymous draughtsman continues with two drawings of a young woman dressed like a frilled pagoda in eight tiers or storeys, at shoulder, elbow, wrist, and waist, and four flounces to her crinoline, which is full, rather than hooped, and, disappointingly, of a black-purplish hue. But we admire her little white lace collar, white lace cuffs, brown gloves to match the brown bows and ribbons on her dress, and the blue handkerchief she holds in one hand, while, with the other, she lifts up three tiers or flounces of her skirt, in front, to show her white lace petticoat, white stockings, and black kid bootees. Next, a scene of fashionable archery at Gosport in the Isle of Wight. Three ladies in " shooting dress ", all wearing similar gloves and hats, and with quivers on belts at their right hips. The butt stands in the distance, and two gentlemen are in attendance ; one, a semi-Highlander, for this undoubted Scotch laird wears tartan trousers, a yellow coat, and a bonnet, a Glengarry tied with ribbons, and has red hair and whiskers. The other wears trousers and a long coat of purplish-violet colour, quiver on his left hip, field glasses on his right, and for fantasy a white topee or sun helmet with a pale-blue ribbon. *Régate de Folkestone* is inscribed below the drawing on the page following. It depicts the back view of a lady in a long purplish mantle draped upon her white flounced crinoline, her hair worn in a chignon, and a round tambour hat ; and a gentleman talking to two women, one in a hat exactly that of the young woman in *Kleptomania*, with a light-blue sunshade on her shoulder, and her companion, who is a dwarf no higher than her elbow, dressed in a white hat and skirt with bright red bobbins.

After this come some miscellaneous drawings, a butcher at Weymouth, a town crier, some Bluecoat boys, a fisherman, a Welsh woman in a top hat, and then the nigger minstrels, *Mr Poppy* playing the bones, in a white shirt and tie, white stockings, black breeches with white braid, and a black-and-white belt, in fact, the beginnings of a uniform for nigger minstrels. *Mr Poppy*, on another page, dancing, but in pink-and-white striped shirt, and wearing a coat with long and thin blue-striped tails to give accent to his high kicks and steps. Last of all, *Comiques Américains*, a more finished drawing. A coon, or black man dancing the cakewalk, in yellow trousers and long blue tail coat, a straw hat, and blue spectacles, holding by the hand a coal-black ballerina who wears red shoes and a bright red ballet skirt. She wears pearl bracelets and necklaces on her black skin, and her hair is braided in a net of pearls. A drawing of a Hogarthian milk-woman, with her yoke and pails, and we are back in London.

Not only in London, but so entirely in the mood and spirit of the moment that, as though he, too, the anonymous Frenchman, has just come out of the music hall, we meet in a bar in the Haymarket at midnight. It is the rendezvous we promised in the beginning, but delayed for a little trifle of four years, for the date is 1868, not 1864. But this makes no difference. It is here and now, with the immediacy of something, remembered in detail, that happened six, or was it seven, years ago. A bar, we remark, in the complete spirit of a public bar, but without the glasses, for the artist has not had time to put them in. An interior that would appeal particularly to a foreigner because it is so English. There are subtle differences in nationality between this sketch — it is no more than that — and Manet's wonderful painting of *Le Bar aux Folies-Bergère*. That is, in glorification, the array of bottles behind the counter in a *bistro*. Even so, it may be suspected that the bar was installed in the Paris music hall as an importation direct from London, and it is not improbable that the barmaid in the painting was an Englishwoman. But the comparison between a little sketch and a great masterpiece must be pursued no further. We will only suggest that Manet himself would have been more interested in this drawing, and in the three that follow, than in a watercolour by Birket Foster.

Two soldiers are talking to the pair of barmaids. But it is, in fact, the merest sketch. All we have is the bulbous part of the bar with its row of upright handles. At the back there is the usual mirror, and a pair of light-blue curtains looped up with cords. But the bar, the curtains, and the mirror have the effect of an altar, or, rather, of an altar rail. It is a barrier, and the sacred beings inhabit the space behind it, a confined territory which has its exit from underneath the counter. The two soldiers wear uniforms, one of red, and one of blue. The latter, a cavalryman belonging, probably, to a regiment of Lancers, for he wears the Lancer's round cap, leans with an elbow on the counter and faces in our direction. He has the pomaded hair and whiskers of the day. The other and more imposing figure comes from the Foot Guards. He wears dark trousers and a scarlet coat, not a pea-jacket like his companion, but a coat of curious length, for it comes down to between his waist and knees. A dark crimson sash passes over his left shoulder and is knotted on his other hip, giving an air of importance to him so that we are to understand he is a recruiting sergeant ; he holds a long stick in his hand as he stands with his back to us at the bar, and has a little round red cap with a white band riding on his great head of hair.

The barmaids have, already, something of the Babylonian priestesses who ply their trade outside, along the lamp-lit pavement. Only, as we shall see, they are bigger in physique, being English, not Belgian or French women, but of a race or breed apart, London barmaids, who are as much a type to themselves as the giant wrestlers in Japan. Their characteristic is a florid charm, and now, eighty years later, we might look for it in vain, or find it nearly gone. One of them, one of the priestesses, stands at her altar. We only see the mustard-yellow top of her dress, worn with a large brooch or cameo, and her low neck and shoulders, for she is dressed as though for the ball. Her chestnut hair is worn in long curls or ringlets, she wears a necklace, and her face is heavily rouged and painted. Her colleague stands, not facing us, but to one side, so that we see her extraordinary and elaborate headdress. Her gown is green, to set off her auburn hair, which is bound with green ribbons, falls in cascades upon the back of her neck and bosom, and even then is luxuriant enough to be gathered into a great casque or protuberance like the headdresses of the Sassanian kings in the rock sculptures, so that, in dimension only, it is as though she has two heads, one behind or above the other. With this she wears a blue necklace and blue earrings and is not less heavily rouged and painted than her sister. Both women have an air of heavy silence clinging to them, which comes from long hours of waiting, but, like all bar-maids, they are quick in repartee, and have a look of insolent boldness or *bravura*. Through the engraved glass windows of this bar in the Haymarket, and in the mirror, we can see the gaslit vortex outside, for in the Haymarket we are at the heart of Babylonian London.

These streets are a favourite haunt with the Frenchman when he is away from his English family, and alone for a day or two in London ; Coventry Street, Windmill Street, all streets leading from the Haymarket towards Leicester Square. He has drawn three scenes or studies of night life, all headed " Haymarket, juillet, 1868 ", but marked " 11^h du soir ", " 1^h du matin ", and " 2^h du matin ". The ' locale ' is the same but a little higher up or lower down the pavement, and in each case outside the glass windows of a public bar or wine shop, and we read the street names at the corner, and " J. W. Cooke, Spirits, Ales, Wines, Ginger Beer ", all painted on the windows, and " French Dinners ", " Divan Turc ", and " Café Turc ".

The first scene, 11^h du soir, is outside the " Divan Turc " and " Café Turc ". It is early in the evening before business, as distinct from the afternoon session, has begun. The priestesses walk in humility before the eye of the law, in the shape of a giant policeman. Were we to see this policeman on an antique vase or painting, for the women so much resemble Babylonians, or indeed, any priestesses of the world of antiquity, we would say he must be a god or warrior from his height, but this is contradicted in his long coat, like the frock coat of a clergyman, and because he carries no arms or weapons. It is the dress of a drunken

74

or orgiastic priest, when regarded with its helmet as some distant echo from the antique world, of a warrior priest keeping order within the temple precincts, in the set boundaries which are, in fact, the limits of his beat, say, in the space between Leicester Square and Piccadilly Circus. This drama of the pavement is, at the moment, a parade of innocence and demureness, for it is not possible that the policeman does not know the pair of prostitutes and could not report upon them to police headquarters. They have the look of being newly arrived, probably from lodgings in Soho, from somewhere within walking distance, since there is no tube or omnibus to bring them to their work. Or, no doubt, evidence could be collected from the cab-drivers who stopped and picked up their fares, and drove into the nebulous, the gaseous flares of London, brightening, burning heartlessly into incandescence.

The débutantes, for so it is implied in their walk, are dressed, one in violet, and one in green. But, in fact, they have separated and now pass one another upon their beat. The policeman, with his slow walk, stands between them. He faces the one dressed in violet with long auburn ringlets, and the crown of her hair reaches only to his shoulder. Her dress has great ruches or flounces at her sleeves, and at the hem ; and not a crinoline, but a protuberance at the back which is the beginning of a bustle. Upon the front of her hair she wears a little lace cap, more like an apron, but concealing nothing of the great mass of fronds above it ; a fringe of curls upon her forehead ; a green ribbon binding her curls below the auburn headdress of her own hair ; and three long twisted pigtails down her back to her waist. She has bright-red satin shoes, earrings of sham pearls, and a much-painted face. Her gloved hands are held demurely in front of her, she looks innocently towards the policeman, and we might wonder for what purpose this curiously

dressed young woman is walking in the Haymarket at eleven
o'clock at night. Behind him, with downcast eyes, walks
an even smaller, almost dwarf-like, woman dressed in green.
In green, with a long train which it must be difficult not
to allow to be trodden upon by passers-by, and as well, her
whole dress is a mass of flounces and loose edges. Its outline
is, as it were, frizzled, and exactly resembling the feathering
of the breed of poultry which has that name, a peculiarity
which is as though each plume was combed upwards and a
little backwards, and which in her dress is the effect of so
much feathering and crimping of the green satin. She
has a bodice of spotted muslin, and indeed the green satin
of her dress ends just below her knee in order to show
her spotted muslin underskirt frothing and billowing for
the whole length of her train, and her green satin shoes.
A dress that makes a considerable noise and rustling upon
the pavement and that can only be worn upon a summer
evening, a dress suitable for a temple dancer or a priestess
of Cybele, and that, with its flounces and its long train to
sweep from side to side, suggests the flounced skirts of the
Gaditanians, who danced with castanets and were famed
" for their agility of body and incontinency ". This creature,
with dyed and painted face and shrewish features, has a
terrible *toupée* or mop of peroxide hair and, to match, a
necklace of amber beads, while the front of her forehead
sports a ridiculous flat straw hat, like a plate or disk, kept
in place by a red ribbon, matching her gloves, and tied in
a bow at the back of her head. Her demeanour, with downcast eyes looking at the pavement, is that of a person who has
gone for a quick walk in order to think, or of someone who
is walking for the sake of exercise. In another moment she
will pass by and catch up with the policeman, and walk
straight on, looking neither to the right nor left, and take the
near corner and be gone from sight, while her companion

with the violet dress and auburn ringlets passes under the eye of the policeman and, we may think, has some sort of understanding with him.

In every direction for half a mile the priestesses are at their nocturnal duties. Some instinct tells us that they are French or Belgian, that they have lived in London for four or five years, and in two or three years more will disappear entirely so that they cannot be found. Somewhere, their bones must still be lying ; but where, and in what continent ? What of the shrewish one, with the pointed face and gilded hair ? And we think we catch her shrill voice on the landing, above the dark stair. Or of the other, that we could invite the auburn-haired priestess to a chop-house or a " French dinner " and try, in vain, to make her tell us of her adventures, but she poses as a child of misfortune and an innocent.

So we pass on, in order to lose ourselves in this Babylon around Piccadilly Circus and Leicester Square. There are drunken soldiers and drunken sailors. It is the all-night district. Not a light is turned low, even upon the upper floors. Or we may have had some supper ; but when we return to the Haymarket with the Frenchman it is two hours later. The second of his drawings is dated " 1^h du matin ". We are at the corner of Coventry Street, outside " J. W. Cooke, Spirits, Ales, Wines, Ginger Beer ". Again there are two women and between them, with his back to us, a man in brown with a walking stick, and a heavy, ugly cap. One hand, in nervousness, is thrust deep into his coat pocket as he looks and watches. But this individual is of no importance, even if he speaks to them. The whole interest is in the pair of women.

One of them advances towards us from the left with a particular gait or mode of walking. She has red-gold hair, bound with a red ribbon, red-gold ringlets over her shoulders, red gloves, and red necklace and earrings, and a green dress, but it is a different green from her predecessor of two hours ago, and shaped curiously, like an ant's body, that is to say, it is bulbous but ends prematurely above her knees, like the ghost of a crinoline, and then begins again. A green dress superimposed upon a white foundation, for the lower half of her dress and her whole train are of white, unspotted muslin, much ruched, and ending in a triple tier or row of ruches above the edge of her white petticoat, shown only at her foot, which is in a black shoe with a scarlet heel. The entire dress trembles and falls and rises with her tread, while her outline reminds us of those insects whose bodies are formed, not from two, but from four or more protuberances, one behind another, but all of the same bulbous shape. A queen-ant, it may be, but of a giant or monstrous kind. She wears a black hat, like a man's bowler, upon her red-gold locks, a hat with black ostrich feathers floating on the air, and as she walks forward looking at her own reflection in the window of the public-house, she holds a cigar in her red-gloved hand.

Both women are smoking cigars. This one, at least, holds it in her hand, but the other comes along with her cigar in her mouth, puffing out the smoke. They are smoking on their beat at this late hour of the night, or it is, in fact, the early morning. This other woman wears a dress of white material entirely flecked or spotted with red dots. Nothing but that, and a little hem showing of plain white, but it is, like the others, a dress with a long train. She has brown-auburn hair, and a black tambour hat, flat and round, and riding on her forehead, and blue ostrich feathers. In one hand, like the Infantas of Velasquez, she holds a big cambric handkerchief, and comes forward, walking insolently, puffing her cigar. The hundreds of red dots on her dress, of varying sizes, draw attention to her brazen insolence, for she is like a figure caught in a red snowstorm who refuses to shake

off the flakes, who is even proud of the marks of shame and wears scarlet on white, on purpose, to show her calling.

We pass on, going deeper and deeper into that gaslight Babel, but an hour later are at the corner of Windmill Street. This is the drawing dated " Haymarket 2ʰ du matin ". Getting late, even for London, and it is to be noticed that the younger women have gone. They are no longer the débutantes of " 11ʰ du soir ". Those have vanished upon their assignations. The more mature cigar smokers have gone, too, or will come round no more. Instead, they are older women, or looking so, for they may not be more than in their late thirties, but this means twenty years, a whole generation of experience. They will have been the débutantes, in their turn, in 1848, and one woman, sure enough, wears the fashions of the early 'fifties, a seven-tiered crinoline, but quite different in shape from those worn by the others. She has the waist of her youth, or space where that had been, a cerise sash and great cerise bow, behind, with long ends, and her cuffs and sleeves are of her youth. She even wears a cerise-and-white bonnet which ties under her chin. She has a round face, thick cheeks, thick lips, and dark-brown hair. Her face is painted cherry-coloured to go with her white-and-cerise dress. But she is in a temper. She is furiously agitated and threatens someone with her fan, for is it not a July night in Windmill Street ?

Her companion is the ghost of many known to Concanen, a late reveller of a time when they still dressed like revellers, enjoying himself, too, at a late date in his own life, for he is a gentleman of between fifty and sixty years of age, with greying beard and whiskers. He has a dark straw hat, or ' boater ', of that colour when the straw is nearly green, a straw with a wide band, tilted forward, and he wears an eyeglass on a string. Next, his cigar held in a red-gloved hand, but we are ready to believe it is red dogskin, we can see the black lines upon his knuckles, and we notice his stiff white collar and stiff white cuffs, with links. His coat and trousers are of a thick powder blue, a short coat not much longer than a pea-jacket, and with black braid at his wrists and coat collar, at his pocket and down his trouser leg. In his left hand he holds a jaunty walking stick. The trousers of this ' blue man ' are cut nearly on the line of leggings or of riding breeches, exceedingly tight, that is to say, and giving prominence to his knees, but full again at his ankles and where they touch his shoes. This, and his short coat, have been purposely designed in order to give an accent to the way he walks or stands. His stick and monocle, and the gesture of his cuff and sleeve leading to the long cigar held up in his red-gloved hand, or again, his stiff collar and the way his hair and beard are trimmed, all are conscious personality or the effect that he would like to give. Nothing has been left to chance. Who is he, we wonder ? What is he doing ? He is tall, and, it is obvious, has been a soldier, a cavalry officer in the Crimean War, but he is disputing with a woman at two o'clock in the morning at the corner of Windmill Street. Or is he just talking ? For there is a type of person who will speak to anyone he meets on his way home, who likes walking late at night. But no. She looks up angrily, and makes as though to strike him with her fan.

And the business of the night is not over. Another woman, for it grows chilly on this July night, hurries past, and she, too, is of a certain age. In an elegant black lace shawl draped, Spanish fashion, upon her neck and shoulders and trailing at the back of her dress, like a mantle, almost to the ground, the dress itself white, with many frills and ruches lifted, in front, by a hand in a lemon-coloured glove to show her spotted muslin petticoat. She has profuse yellow hair, fringed like the hair of Henrietta-Maria over her forehead, and with the customary mass or protuberance of hair at the back, but dressed more elaborately than usual with a necklace, it is nothing less, of jet beads binding the crown of her head at the point where the headdress of her own hair begins. Not only this, but an inch or two in front of it she wears a pale-blue ribbon to match her blue drop-earrings, and this ribbon running parallel to her fringe of curls, together with the ringlets of false hair that fall on her neck and upon her bosom, gives the effect of a woman of Carthage, or of Tyre and Sidon. Here, in London, between Piccadilly Circus and Leicester Square, at the corner of Windmill Street, we see walking past us a priestess of Astarte, a goddess who was the Venus of the Phoenicians.

Five of the six women drawn by the Frenchman have these extraordinary headdresses of false hair. The same number have their hair dyed auburn, or tinted with henna or peroxide to sham gold. All five of them wear the coloured ribbons in their hair : the auburn débutante a jade-green ribbon ; the little shrew a ribbon of vermilion to hold her white straw hat in place ; a ribbon of sealing-wax red for the red-gold hair of the first of the cigar smokers in her black billycock, with her ant-like figure dressed in green with white train or wings, holding her cigar in her red-gloved hand ; a dark-blue ribbon for her companion in the red-spotted crinoline ; and now this pale-blue ribbon and necklace, worn as a bandeau, of jet beads. This last of the priestesses wears a little yellow straw hat, tilted well forward and crowned with blue ostrich feathers. They all have their hair dressed in the same fashion. Their curls and ringlets, their headdresses of false hair, it is reasonable to suppose must come off when they untie the ribbons. In fact, these women are wearing headdresses of false hair that are as artificial as a periwig, ceremonial wigs worn for public occasions in the streets of the city, that can be worn for a day or two together, but, more often, will be found upon the dressing-table in the morning. Their hats, too, are chosen from the same family. A hat like a little white lace apron worn on that auburn crown as though its wearer wore nothing else, but she is dressed from head to foot in violet ; the little hat of white straw ; the black billycock with black ostrich feathers ; the black tambour with blue ostrich plumes ; the yellow straw hat with fine blue feathers.

Probably no one but a Frenchman would have understood the subtle differences, or been able to draw their hats and dresses and the details of their hair. It is apparent, perhaps, that he is concerned with his own countrywomen, and that they are emigrants from Paris or from Brussels, yet they are as dyed and painted as Levantines and call to mind the priestesses of Carthage or of Tyre and Sidon. They are crinolined like Minoan goddesses in tiered skirts, or they wear trains or cages. Immodesty has its opportunity in rouge and paint and vulgar colours, and in other respects they are dressed but a year or two behind the fashions. That, as an artist, the Frenchman was but an amateur is shown clearly in his three drawings, for most of the characters are drawn in profile. But where, as a witness, he is invaluable is in the details of their clothes and headdresses, and looking at them we may ask ourselves what more improbable figures have ever been seen than in utilitarian London. They are only two generations later in date than Utamaro's beauties of the Yoshiwara, and those, indeed, are their only equivalent. These women, one and all, will have been born in the beginnings of the railway age, and the oldest of them may have left her home by diligence to embark on the great city, Antwerp, Lyons, Brussels, Paris — and then London. Where will they end ? For in another decade it is improbable that a single one of them will be still living. It is curious, though, to reflect that if, as we surmise, the auburn-haired débutante of the first drawing was a Belgian, and perhaps fifteen years old, not more, at the time of our seeing her, according to Belgian law, which does not presume the death of persons who have disappeared from home until they reach the age of a hundred years, this priestess of the pavement of Windmill Street in the summer of 1868 is still legally alive, being no more than ninety-four years old, a not unheard-of age. In an attic somewhere, or back on the farm among the cocks and hens ? Within sound of the *pavé*, where wooden shoes still clatter on the cobbles ? Among her grandchildren and great-grandchildren ? Or boxed up, years ago, and thrown into the common grave ? Who can tell ?

And in another moment we are in the quiet streets and out of the bright lights and the hum and roar of traffic. Along Piccadilly it never ceases, all night, and into the early morning. But we are in one of the backwaters and walking home. In another hour the market carts with fruit and vegetables will begin trotting past to Covent Garden. Another sort of traffic and the dawn of yet one more July day. By now, the last of the characters of our *Morning, Noon and Night in London* will be abed, scattered to the four winds of the metropolis, but to meet again next morning or early in the afternoon. The young beau of *The Hansom Galop* or *The Age of Paper*, where will he be lying ? In one of the new bachelors' flats in Victoria Street, or in the family house in Eaton Square ? And the two young women of *Kleptomania* ? Living together, perhaps, in a little stucco villa in Maida Vale ? With the rent paid for them by a protector, and even now, in their dreams, plotting and planning for tomorrow ?

And *The Bond Street Beau* ? Here it occurs to us that we could meet him, day after day, year after year, in the same part of Bond Street, and then making his turn and coming back again, but with unaccountable absences of a few weeks at a time. Gone for a holiday to the seaside? No; holidaying, free of expense, in a quiet part of London. He lives "in digs"; but where, exactly? However, we have not to worry, for we remember that he is but a stage character. Yet this is not true. He is the prototype of more than one person. He resumes them all. We even watch him growing older, but all through the years we shall never know his name or address. He is a phantom haunting us in daylight. We have only to look for him, and he is there. And *The Dark Girl Dress'd in Blue*? Where, and with whom, is she adventuring? But she is a year or two older. Crinolines are out of fashion. We met her that once, or twice, and will never set eyes on her again. Vanished absolutely, and there is no one of whom we can ask her name. And Concanen himself? We know so little of him that we cannot say. Certainly he has not had his due. Of our other witness, the Frenchman, we do not even know his name. A French tutor, and that is all. But for an hour or two of a summer night they knew a part of London better than we do ourselves. Eternal London, now a quarter part in ruins, and with pits and gashes everywhere.

But it is finished. There are no more flying bombs. Days and nights have been free of them for a year or more. London is still standing. And we are drawing towards the end of our walk in London. We have passed the Haymarket and Lower Regent Street, Piccadilly and Old Bond Street. The traffic lights are flashing but the street is empty. We have the pavement and the whole road to ourselves. No one is in sight. Those men and women of eighty, ninety, nearly a hundred years ago, would know, even now, that they are in London. For the aspect of London alters, but its spirit never changes. Some few of the same spectres haunt its pavements. Here and now, tonight, or tomorrow.

But the dawn is breaking. Like *The Bond Street Beau* and his friends, whom we meet, and know by sight, but never speak to, we shall fall asleep by daylight. When we wake the day has already begun, and once more, as always, it will be Morning, Noon and Night in London.

NOTE

MR IFAN KYRLE FLETCHER, who has made researches into the life history of Alfred Concanen, kindly supplies the following information. The Concanen family came from the borders of Co. Roscommon and Co. Galway. Alfred Concanen, the designer of music-hall song covers, was born in London in 1835. He was married in a London register office, September 8th, 1858, his address being given as 43 Bloomsbury Street, to Mary Anne Tholen of 1 Kirkmans Place, Tottenham Court Road, a spinster of eighteen years old, her father being Lambert Tholen, described as a driver. Alfred Concanen is described as a lithographer, and his father Edward Concanen as an artist. The death certificate of Alfred Concanen gives the date of his death as November 10th, 1886, and his age as fifty-one. "Short, slight, with a heavy cavalry moustache", he was undoubtedly a personality in the Bohemia of his day. Mr Gordon Craig, in a letter to the donor of these notes, describes a meeting with him in a tavern in the Strand (near the Lyceum Theatre, where Gordon Craig was working at the time with Irving). He tells a characteristic anecdote, and adds that Concanen died that same night of apoplexy, so that Gordon Craig, then a boy of sixteen years old, may have been one of the last persons to see Concanen alive.

In evidence of Concanen's wide powers as a lithographic draughtsman we would draw attention to his coloured print of *The Capture of Magdala*, a scene from the Abyssinian campaign of 1868, one of the finest and latest in date of British military prints, taken from the sketch of an officer present, and set in a rocky landscape reminiscent of the peaks of Meteora.

S. S.

PRINTED BY R. & R. CLARK, LTD., EDINBURGH